Contents

Introduction

Some people catch on to what sex is about pretty early. By the time they're in their teens, they act like miniature sex gurus, dispensing wisdom left, right and centre. Everyone knows someone like this; you may even have gone to them for advice. The problem is, if you don't know anything about sex, how do you know their advice is right? I remember a friend's sister telling us that a girl couldn't get pregnant the first time she had sex, as long as the boy was a virgin too. Unfortunately, she later discovered she wasn't as clued-up as she thought.

I was pretty lucky when it came to sex education. My mother was a nurse, so talking about sex was pretty open and matter of fact in our household. But most of my friends weren't so lucky. One friend was brought up to believe only 'bad' girls had sex because it was 'dirty' and 'wrong', something she still struggles with today. And one boy I knew got all his information from his elder brother's porn collection and ended up with a pretty distorted view of what sex was all about.

Even though sex education has become more readily available, many people still aren't told enough about sex. Some adults are too embarrassed to talk to young people about sex. Others won't discuss it, as they believe that telling young people about sex encourages them to do it. We all know this is a load of rubbish, but that doesn't stop them trying to make sure teenagers don't see anything provocative.

If you don't know anything about sex and puberty, you owe it to yourself to find out. Some of you might be too shy to ask questions; others won't like to admit they're confused, for fear of losing face. The fact is, no-one will think you're weird for trying to find out about sex. People will, however, think you're foolish if you ignore all the warnings and rush into it without thinking. Remember, sex is a big deal and you can get hurt if you don't educate yourself, so do yourself a favour and start reading. *

Anita

* For any terms or phrases you don't understand, turn to the glossary on page 124 for an explanation.

CHAPTER ONE

Your changing body

Welcome to puberty

Do you feel tearful one minute and wonderfully happy the next? Miserable because your once together body has suddenly started curving in all sorts of directions? Are you suddenly obsessed with the boy down the street, the one you used to really loathe? Do you have a desire to be grown-up one minute, and curled up in your mum's lap the next? If you do, don't worry, you're not going mad, you're going through puberty!

What is puberty?

Welcome to one of the hardest times of your life. Puberty is the stage where you turn both physically and mentally from a child into an adult. This doesn't mean that you're going to go to sleep measuring 4' 5" (1.4m) and wake up the next day measuring 5' 8" (1.8m) – puberty will take time to work its way through your body: about five or six years in fact, which, translated, means a good few years of turmoil. For some people the changes that puberty brings are greeted with joy:

"When I started my periods I was so happy. I thought they were never going to start because all my friends came on months before."

Gilly (13)

"I had the flattest chest ever. The boys would call me 'fried egg', then one day I noticed they'd grown. Not hugely, but enough to stop all the stupid jokes."

Anna (13)

"I used to be quite small and people used to pick on me because of my size. Then I suddenly grew. Now I feel like a different person and no-one bullies me."

Jack (14)

For others, the changes puberty brings aren't so rewarding:

"I used to have good skin. Now look at it: pimples and spots everywhere! I look disgusting. When I see pictures of me a year ago, I want to cry. It's so unfair."

Lisa (12)

"Ever since I started growing I've put on weight. My mum says it's just puppy fat, but I hate it. I'm all lumpy and nothing I do gets rid of it."

Gemma (13)

"I have all these spots and facial hair. I know I look pretty ugly. What girl would ever look twice at me?"

Mike (14)

Just how puberty will affect you is hard to say. You might find your best friend starts their growth spurt a good two years before you, or you might find yourself the first person in your class with a period. It's even hard to say how tall you'll end up or how big your bust will be. If you want a rough idea, take a look at your mum and dad. Certain things about your body

will be determined by their biological make-up – for example, if both your parents are small with brown hair, it's unlikely (but not definite, thanks to their parents and their parents' parents) that you'll be 6ft with blonde hair! If you're at all curious about how your body will change and when it will start happening, try asking your parents when they first noticed their bodies growing. This will give you a pretty good indication of what to expect.

What happens during puberty?

Puberty is a time of rapid growth for both boys and girls. Your body changes shape, your reproductive system matures and you'll develop other sexual characteristics, such as pubic hair (hair which grows on your genital area). The process takes between three and five years, but can be longer or shorter than this.

During puberty, girls can expect:

- Breast development
- Pubic hair
- A growth spurt
- Hips to widen, producing a more curvy shape
- The formation of adult sweat glands, which leads to more body sweat and body odour
- Periods
- Armpit hair
- Spots
- More body fat

During puberty, boys can expect:

- The testes (balls) to grow
- Pubic hair
- Active sweat glands
- A growth spurt
- To ejaculate semen (or to 'come')
- Facial hair
- Spots
- The voice will 'break' (the voice will become deeper as the voice box enlarges).

Why does puberty happen?

It is our hormones which are responsible for puberty. These are chemicals released from the brain that stimulate the growth and development of our bodies and sex organs.

At around the age of 10 in girls and 12 in boys, a master hormone is released by the pituitary gland at the base of the brain. This hormone activates specific sex hormones in your body, which will make your sexual organs grow. In boys, this sex hormone is called testosterone and in girls, oestrogen. Testosterone is the hormone behind the production of sperm and oestrogen is the hormone behind the development of breasts and the start of periods.

Hormones cause all sorts of other changes in the body, including mood swings which may make you feel angry, sad, miserable or depressed. The fact is, it can take quite a while for your hormones to settle down and find the correct balance, which is why you might feel odd for a while.

Puberty and boys

What's what?

- The **penis** lengthens and thickens during puberty, but this is a slow process and won't happen overnight. Your penis will get longer before it gets wider. Some boys get hung up on the size of their penis, but remember that all penises are different. Some are thick, some are long, some are thin, some bend slightly in one direction.

It's important to remember that everyone matures at a different rate and boys of the same age rarely have the same size penis until the end of puberty. Once they are fully mature, most boys' penises are actually the same size when erect, whatever size they are when flaccid (not erect). Penis size is not an indication of anything, it's just like having big or small feet.

- The **foreskin** is the skin fold covering the end of the penis. Boys who have been circumcised have had the foreskin removed for religious or medical reasons.

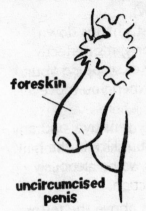 

foreskin

uncircumcised penis

circumcised penis

- The **scrotum** is the bag of skin that holds the testicles behind the penis. Around puberty the scrotum gets bigger and turns a slightly different colour. Contrary to popular myth, 'balls' or testes do not just suddenly drop into the scrotum, they descend gradually. You may also notice some small dots on the skin of your scrotum: don't worry about these. They are points from which pubic hair will grow, and are nothing to worry about.

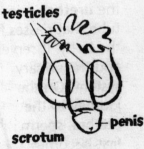

testicles

penis

scrotum

- The **testicles** are where sperm will eventually be produced. They are made up of two parts, the **testes** (balls) and the **epididymis**, a coiled tube that surrounds each testis (ball). When sperm is produced by the testes, it passes into the epididymis until it reaches maturity and starts moving (after about 20 days). Once the sperm are mature they pass to the next part of the reproductive system (see below).

If you've noticed that one testis hangs down lower than the other, don't worry, it's perfectly normal and is your body's way of stopping your testes pressing on each other when you move around.

Remember, the testes are very sensitive, and any knock can be extremely painful. A kick in the balls may seem like a joke, but it's a way of seriously damaging someone.

- The **vas deferens** are the tubes above the testes where mature sperm are stored and then passed to the **urethra** prior to ejaculation. The urethra is a tube that passes from the bladder to the outside of the body. It serves both the reproductive system and the urinary system. On the journey to the urethra, sperm first becomes mixed with fluid (partly fructose, a sugar which provides fuel for the sperm to swim) from the **seminal vesicles** and

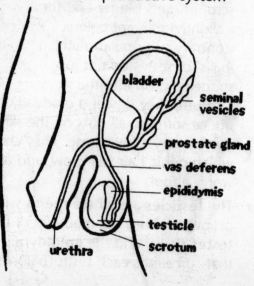

bladder

seminal vesicles

prostate gland

vas deferens

epididymis

testicle

scrotum

urethra

the **prostate gland**, both found near the bladder. This mixture is known as **semen**.

- An **erection** is the name given to an aroused penis. When a boy is sexually aroused, his limp penis will fill with blood and grow bigger and stiffer. Around puberty boys find themselves getting erections at awkward moments, even when they're not thinking about sex, like on the bus or in lessons. As untimely and embarrassing as this is, it's also completely normal and happens to all boys at this time.

erection

What happens during an erection?

- When a boy is sexually aroused, blood flows into the penis, while sperm moves into the vas deferens and then to the prostate gland, where it mixes with fluid to make up semen.

- **Ejaculation** is the release of semen out of the erect penis as a result of sexual excitement. Ejaculations don't start in boys until the onset of puberty, though erections are present from birth. Usually a boy's first ejaculation is at night and is known as a wet dream.

- **Wet dreams** are ejaculations that happen while boys are asleep. They're irritating because they can't be controlled, predicted, or stopped. Wet dreams occur mainly at the beginning of puberty and are the body's way of releasing sexual tension.

Puberty and girls

What's what?

- The first sign of puberty for most girls is growing **breasts**. When these first start to develop they are known as breast buds. Nipples will grow larger and breasts may feel sensitive and tender. It's important to know that breasts grow at different rates. This is why you may notice one breast is larger than the other at first. This is perfectly normal, so try not to worry about it, as over time your breasts will equal out and become relatively the same size (though one will always be slightly larger than the other).

- Unlike boys, the majority of the female sex organs are inside the female body. Female sex organs are known collectively as the **vulva**. This includes the mons pubis, the vaginal lips, the clitoris and the vaginal vestibule.

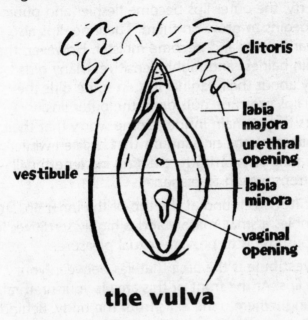

clitoris

labia majora

urethral opening

labia minora

vaginal opening

vestibule

the vulva

- The **mons pubis** is the only part of the vulva that can be seen from the outside. It is the fleshy part covering your pubic bone. During puberty this area becomes more prominent and is covered with pubic hair.

mons pubis

- The **vaginal lips** – known as the **labia majora** (outer lips) and the **labia minora** (inner lips) – are made up of fatty tissue and contain numerous oil and sweat glands that moisten the vulva, preventing it from getting dry and sore. During puberty, the outer lips become fleshier and pubic hair begins to grow on them. The inner lips also appear fleshier and become moister. However, they remain hairless and highly sensitive. Many girls worry about their vaginal lips. In some girls the inner lips protrude outside of the outer lips, in others they remain inside. Some worry that their lips are too large or hang down, but like every other part of your body, the size and length will vary from person to person.

- The **clitoris** is found at the top of the inner lips. It resembles a small marble and is highly sensitive. Its sole purpose is to provide sexual pleasure.

- The **vestibule** is the area that lies between your inner lips. At the front of this area is your urethral opening, where urine exits from the body. Behind this is the vaginal opening, which may be partly covered by the **hymen**, a thin layer of skin which is easily broken during sex or through sport.

- Inside the body is the **vagina**. This is a muscular tube with several functions. It carries menstrual flow from the uterus, serves as a birth canal during pregnancy, and is where the penis is placed during sex. During puberty the vagina becomes longer and wider. At the upper end of the vagina you'll find the **cervix** (neck of the uterus). Around puberty the cervix and the vagina begin to produce **discharge**, a fluid which is usually clear or white in colour. This is nothing to worry about. This secretion of mucus and fluid is a way of cleaning out the vagina. Some girls find their discharge changes colour a few days before their period. If it is itchy or smells bad, it could mean you have an infection. Most women get vaginal infections from time to time, but they are normally easily cleared up with medical help. If you're at all worried, get it checked out by your doctor. As for vaginal smells, don't use vaginal deodorants or douches. It is completely normal and natural for your vagina to have a musky smell to it.

- Two tubes lead off the uterus and these are called the **fallopian tubes**. At the top of these are the **ovaries**, where the eggs or **ovum** are stored. When a girl is born, her ovaries contain between 3 to 4 million unripe eggs.

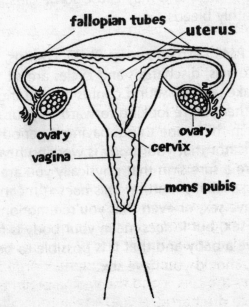

fallopian tubes

uterus

ovary

ovary

vagina

cervix

mons pubis

By the time her first period comes along, this number has reduced to about 500,000 (the other eggs are re-absorbed into the body). Ovaries become larger during puberty as they start to respond to hormones released from the brain. As they grow, they produce the sex hormone, oestrogen, which activates the growth of all the other sexual organs. This causes the unripe eggs to ripen. When this occurs, one egg a month is released from the ovaries (known as **ovulation**) travelling down the fallopian tubes into the uterus.

Periods

Periods, menstruation, being on, the curse, monthlies – the list of names associated with periods is endless and may cause some girls to dread their monthly bleeds.

Likewise, PMS (also known as PMT), cramps, tampons, sanitary towels, discharges and cycles are all terms which make periods sound confusing and frightening, but, whether you're looking forward to your period or not, bear in mind one thing: having a period is a good indicator that your body is working healthily. Periods are a sure sign that physically you are becoming sexually mature. This *doesn't* mean that you should have sex, or even that you're emotionally ready for sex, but it *does* mean your body is now set up to have a baby and that it is possible to become pregnant, should you have sex.

What is a period?

A period occurs each month as the body prepares itself for a possible pregnancy. An egg is released from one of the ovaries and travels down the fallopian tubes to the uterus. While the egg moves down the tube, the uterus prepares for the egg's arrival by lining its walls with tissue. If the egg is not fertilised by joining up with a sperm (which it won't be if sex hasn't taken place) the lining breaks down and starts to flush itself out. A period is, therefore, a mixture of blood (2–3 tablespoons, though it looks much more) uterus lining and fluid. Periods can last for up to five days, sometimes more.

Menarche

A girl's first period is known as menarche and can start at any age. It usually begins after your breasts and pubic hair have grown, though this very much depends on your own personal body clock. The exact time you begin your periods will be dictated by your hormones and genetic make-up.

Regular and irregular periods

Once you've started, don't expect your periods to begin at the same time every month. For the first two years, your periods are likely to be irregular, and sometimes non-existent. This is completely normal because periods take time to regulate. As your ovaries mature, your periods will probably fall into a 28 day cycle (sometimes longer, sometimes shorter).

Counting your cycle

A cycle begins from the first day you start your period, for instance, if you begin bleeding on the 15th of January, you count 28 days on from then, which makes the projected start of your next period (the first day you actually bleed), the 12th day of February.

Pains, PMS and what to do

It is estimated that 90% of women suffer from PMS (Pre-Menstrual Syndrome) and period pain at some point in their lives. PMS is caused by hormones, and sufferers may find themselves with a variety of symptoms including: bloating, moodiness, spots, tearfulness and headaches, to name but a few.

Help yourself by:

- Eating a healthy diet, making sure you eat lots of fresh fruit and vegetables.
- Cutting out sugar, fizzy drinks, coffee and fatty foods. All these things slow down your digestive system and can make an uncomfortable period feel even worse.

Period pain or cramps are thought to be contractions of the muscles in the uterus as they push the uterus lining out.

Help yourself by:

- Placing a hotwater bottle on your stomach, which will help to relax the muscles.

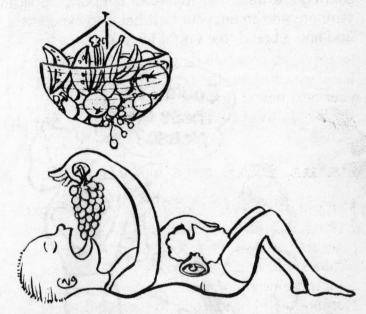

- Exercising. This may be the last thing you feel like doing, but exercise releases endorphins (the body's natural painkillers) which will help to relieve period pain.
- Eating healthily.
- You can buy painkillers at the chemist which should help, but check with your pharmacist or doctor before you start taking them.

Which sanitary protection should I use?

One of the most confusing things about periods is choosing what kind of sanitary protection to use. With the market awash with billions of types, such as panty liners, thin towels, ordinary towels, overnight towels, non-applicator tampons, applicator tampons and so on, your best bet is to experiment and find a brand that's right for you.

By all means take advice from friends and mothers, but at the end of the day, choose something that feels right for you.

Tampons

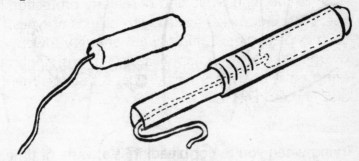

Myth: Only women who have had sex can use tampons.
Any girl having a period can use tampons. Tampons are rolls of cotton wool with a string attached to one end. They are either inserted using a cardboard or plastic applicator or by pushing the tampon in with a finger. When inserted into the vagina, the string hangs down outside the vaginal lips, enabling you to remove a soiled tampon easily. Ignore all stories about tampons being lost inside you. This is impossible and if you ever have trouble removing a tampon, your doctor or a practice nurse at your local surgery can do it quickly and efficiently for you.

Most girls find tampons hard to use the first time they try them. Often tampons are hard to insert because the muscles in the vagina are too tense, or your hymen is still intact. If this is the case, then stop trying and have another go when you feel less anxious. It might be useful to use a slender tampon which has the same absorbency as a regular tampon, but is extra slim, so can be easily inserted. Remember, only insert a tampon when you're on your period.

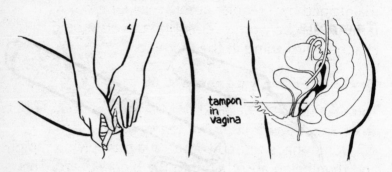

tampon
in
vagina

Trying when you're not bleeding is a waste of time, because the vagina is far too dry. Make sure you use a tampon of the right absorbency (either regular, super or super plus, depending on how heavy your period flow is) and change it regularly (usually every four to eight hours).

Needing to change a regular tampon in less than four hours is a sign you need a higher absorbency tampon. However, you will only need to use super tampons on certain days of your period, as blood flow is heavier on some days and lighter on others.

Some women say they feel a slight bubbling sensation when their tampon needs changing. This sensation is blood flow and shows that the tampon is no longer absorbing the blood. If you don't feel this, you can still easily tell whether a tampon needs changing by a quick visit to the bathroom. While leakage does occur with tampons, blood never comes gushing out, and will only trickle slightly.

Remember, using a super tampon doesn't mean you can keep it in longer than a regular tampon, they are only for girls who have heavy flows that can't be maintained by a regular absorbency tampon. A tampon can be worn overnight, but you should change it first thing in the morning.

Toxic Shock Syndrome

You may notice a warning on your tampon box about Toxic Shock Syndrome. This is a very, very rare syndrome that's caused by bacteria multiplying rapidly and then being absorbed into the bloodstream. This can happen if bacteria grows on a tampon, which is one of the reasons why it's important to change your tampons regularly. If you feel at all uncomfortable, sick or dizzy, remove your tampon.

Sanitary towels

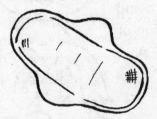 

Myth: Everyone can tell you're wearing one.
These days most towels are so thin, no-one will ever notice you are wearing one. Many girls feel happier with sanitary towels, and, despite what people say, they are not unhygienic, as long as you change them regularly. Work out which towel is best for you by trying a variety of brands. Nearly all come in discreet packaging, with adhesive strips to attach them to your

knickers. The downside of using towels is that they can leak more obviously than tampons, especially if they slip to one side or if you forget to change them. However, towels with adhesive 'wings' to hold them in place can help to avoid this. Remember to always dispose of sanitary towels properly. Wherever possible, wrap them in toilet paper or in a bag and put them in a special sanitary or outside bin. If all else fails, most are flushable, though this isn't a very environmentally-friendly option.

Breasts

Breasts are a normal part of being a woman. The main function of the breast is, of course, to feed a baby, so the breasts are largely made up of fatty deposits and glands that will produce milk once you've given birth.

Try not to feel self-conscious about your breasts. All breasts are different – some are large, some are small, some droop, some bounce. Whatever you have, and whatever you feel about them, your breasts are *normal*.

Help yourself by:

- Wearing the right bra size. Don't squeeze yourself into one that is too small for you, this will be uncomfortable and look unattractive. Bigger breasts need to be supported properly, as do growing breasts.

- Getting measured. Go along to any major department store and make sure you are fitted for a bra by a trained member of staff. It sounds embarrassing but it's not. It's done in private and you will be measured beneath your breasts and across your breasts to determine your chest and cup size.

Don't panic if you can't fill a bra. There is no set age for your breasts to start developing. Some girls start developing breasts as young as 10 years old while others don't start till they are 16. If you can't fill an adult bra, go for a teen bra.

No devices or special creams can increase breast size, so don't waste your money. Breasts are made up of body fat and glands, not muscles, so any exercises you do will only affect the muscles underneath your breasts.

Having a small chest doesn't mean you're not sexy. Theories that boys only like girls with big breasts are utter rubbish.

Just because you have two breasts, it doesn't mean they will both be identical. Each breast may differ slightly from the other and sometimes during puberty you might find that one is larger than the other. If this is the case, don't worry – the smaller breast will eventually catch up to be a similar size, although they may not be exactly the same.

Lumpy breasts are also very normal during puberty. In fact, breasts are naturally sometimes more lumpy than others, especially around the time of your period. A lump doesn't automatically mean cancer. In fact, breast cancer is very rare below the age of 30 years old.

Universal puberty signs

Male and female body bits aside, there are a number of things puberty brings that are common to both sexes. It's guaranteed that if you're going through puberty you're going to have to cope with one, or all, of these.

Spots

Everyone gets spots at some point in their lives. Sadly, most of us seem to get them just when we could really do without them, particularly during adolescence, a time when we tend to be very sensitive about how we look.

Contrary to popular belief, spots have nothing to do with chocolate, chips or how clean you are. The majority of spots, especially red, lumpy ones, are in fact caused by hormones, which is why they appear when you're stressed and worried and, if you're a girl, around the time of your period. These kinds of spots are known as acne. At puberty your hormones activate your oil glands (sebaceous glands), which may start to over-produce. The glands may become enlarged on your face, back and chest and start secreting an oily substance (sebum) which then plugs up the gland outlet, causing a spot.

The good news is that acne does eventually clear up - but you don't have to suffer in silence until then. Your doctor can help, as can the Acne Support Group, after all, acne is a medical condition, so your doctor can give you medication to help.

Try not to pick your spots. This only spreads them, causes scars and makes them look worse. Don't buy miracle spot products either, as they are a waste of money.

Growing pains

These are painful twinges and pains that may suddenly

strike around your body. The most common places are the back, the legs and the arms. They shouldn't last more than a few minutes and usually they happen at night. Some experts say they are to do with the growth spurt, others disagree. However, everyone agrees they are nothing to worry about, unless your pains are persistent or you get muscle cramps, when you should see your doctor and get them checked out.

Stretch marks

You might grow so quickly during puberty that your skin loses some of its elasticity. If this happens you might find yourself with stretch marks on your skin. These look like pale pink, purple or white lines. They are known medically as 'striae' and do eventually fade in colour, though faint lines will remain. Boys often find them on their buttocks, backs and arms, whilst girls find them on their breasts, stomachs and legs.

Body odour

Puberty also affects your sweat glands. As your body matures, so will the glands under your arms and around your groin. These glands will start to produce a stronger kind of sweat. This is why it's essential you wash every day and keep these areas clean, otherwise you will develop body odour, also known as BO. Body odour occurs when sweat (which *doesn't* smell) hits the air and mixes with bacteria. When it dries on your body or your clothes, it becomes stale and this is what makes you smell.

Apart from washing regularly, you can help yourself by wearing clean cotton clothes. For people who sweat a lot, an anti-perspirant deodorant (products just marked deodorant only mask body odour) can also be helpful.

Pubic and body hair

It's not just boys who notice hair growing on their bodies and faces. Some girls might notice fine hairs growing below their lips or around their nipples. Never ever pluck, shave or use depilatory creams on hair around the nipples, as this area is highly sensitive and prone to infections in the hair follicles. The hair here is usually so fine that only you will notice it, but if it's thicker and you hate it you could always trim it very gently.

With female facial hair, you must never ever shave, or else you'll get stubble. Again, if you can't live with it, try waxing, bleaching or a depilatory cream (available from chemists). Depilatory creams dissolve hair away, but always do a 'spot test' first on a tiny patch of skin to check that you don't react allergically to the product. Underarm hair and leg hair can be shaved or waxed but remember, once you start doing these things you have to continue to do them on a regular basis or else you'll have stubble. The same applies to boys thinking of starting to shave their faces.

Pubic hair starts off quite fine and soft but will become thick, wiry and curly. It may be darker than the hair on your head. At this stage, some women like to remove their pubic hair around their knicker line (also known as the 'bikini line'). Depilatory creams especially for the bikini-line are available from chemists. The hair in this area can also be waxed or shaved (carefully!). Remember, pubic hair is completely natural and everyone – males, females, your parents, your teachers, the bus conductor – has it!

Low self-esteem

Low self-esteem can happen for all kinds of reasons. Maybe you hate the way you look, or suddenly feel shy about your new body. Perhaps you've put on weight (very natural during puberty) and feel unhappy about it. Or maybe you've become really tall and thin and feel like you're towering over everyone else. Maybe you have *all* of the above signs of puberty and just feel overwhelmed by everything.

Help yourself by:

- Not comparing yourself to others. We are all individuals, who develop and grow at different stages. What's normal for you may not be normal for somebody else.
- Eat healthily and exercise, this will make you feel good about yourself and your body.
- Talk about how you feel. Keeping your fears and anxieties locked up inside will only make you feel worse. Find a friend, parent or adult you trust, or try confiding in a diary.
- If you are at all worried, see your doctor (you don't have to go along with your parent).

Even if you've been afflicted with every sign of puberty, don't despair. Puberty doesn't go on forever. Your body and emotions *will* settle down, and you will find a balance you can live with.

Puberty isn't a sign that you're ready to have sex, just as learning to walk isn't a sign that you're ready to run a marathon. Puberty is just a sign that your body is maturing. You don't need to rush into thinking about sex. Just as you have to wait for your body to change, you also have to wait for your feelings to develop.

CHAPTER TWO

Sex education – what's it all about?

Coping with your new body

Puberty changes are bad enough when you have to suffer them in private, but one of the most annoying things about puberty is that everyone suddenly makes it their business. If it's not relatives telling you how much you've grown, then it's fathers, mothers and nosy neighbours commenting on your moods, maturing body and awkward curves. Sometimes it's even friends who make you feel anxiety-ridden!

"The first time I wore a bra, I nearly died of embarrassment. I came downstairs and my mum had obviously told my dad and my grandmother. They all came out to see me and made comments about what a big girl I was turning into. I wanted the ground to open up and swallow me."

Shauna (11)

"My friends all run around in summer with skimpy tops and knickers on. Ever since I started my periods I've felt too self-conscious to do that, so I stay covered up and always refuse to go swimming with them. I worry that my period will suddenly start when I'm in the pool with them."

Nina (12)

"All my friends suddenly look really tall and big, while I'm still small and weedy. They call me shrimp, and I hate it, because it means they think they're better than me. I hate being small like this, and I can't wait for the day I start to grow, but it never seems to happen."

Paul (11)

"The girls in my class call me names behind my back because I've got lots of spots. I know I look terrible, but I don't know what to do. I wash my face every day. I try to cover them up but nothing works. I still look ugly and spotty."

Simon (14)

As if coping with bodily changes isn't bad enough, the subject of sex soon rears its head, not only between friends, but also at home and at school. For some people, it can be quite alarming to have to suddenly start discussing sex before they're even sure what's what.

"My mum came into my room the other night and showed me a condom and some diagrams. I was so embarrassed that I pretended I already knew it all and then tried to make out that I really had to study. But she wouldn't go away and kept saying 'Do you want me to tell you about sex and what happens?' I couldn't even look at her and eventually she went

away. I don't want to hear about sex from my mum – there's
something really creepy about that."

Mike (12)

Sadly, the very subject of sex, periods, erections and
breasts will always cause lots of giggling, because, let's
face it, it's embarrassing to have to discuss these
private things in public. However, you just have to
take a look through the letters on the advice pages of
any magazine to see that there are an awful lot of
half-truths and myths out there when it comes to sex:
dangerous myths that can scare you, or result in you
getting hurt or pregnant.

"The first time I got my period, I thought I was dying.
No-one ever told me about periods. My mum just said
women have these things that come once a month. She
never said it would be blood, and she never said where it
would come from."

Fiona (12)

"I heard that if you kiss someone once you get your
period, you can get pregnant because sperm can be
passed from the mouth and work its way down to your
stomach."

Anne (11)

"The first year I had breasts, I hated them so much that I'd
bandage them down. It was only when my PE teacher
spoke to me, that I confessed what I was doing. She made
me realise that it was normal to have growing breasts.
Until then I had felt so ashamed of them."

Jill (13)

"Just because I'm more developed than everyone else and have a boyfriend, people assume I'm having sex with him. It's just not true. I'm not, I won't even French kiss him."

Wendy (13)

Worries like these are why sex education is so important. It tells you what's normal and what's not, what's truthful and what's not, so you know for sure. Good sex education will help you to understand the mechanics of sex and how having sex is linked to relationships and emotions. It will also help you to see that having sexual feelings doesn't necessarily mean you're ready to have sex.

What is sex education?

The Department of Education states that the aim of sex education should be to: "Prepare pupils to cope with the physical and emotional challenges of growing up, and to give them an elementary understanding of human reproduction."

Some people feel school sex education is a bad idea because they think that talking about sex to young people only encourages them to do it. However, ask any of your friends and the chances are that school wasn't the first place they heard about sex. In fact, you and your friends probably knew a whole lot about the subject long before it ever came up in class. But school sex education means that at least you are getting the facts and not being misinformed by your friends. It's also a good idea if your parents find it difficult to talk to you about personal matters.

What to expect in sex education classes

"I've heard they make you watch a film showing a man and woman having sex. I don't think I could watch that, especially with boys in the room. It would be too embarrassing."

Lisa (12)

"I worry that they're going to make everyone who's started their period put their hands up. That would be too awful. I couldn't tell everyone that I was still waiting for mine."

Helen (12)

Don't be worried about these classes – you won't be asked any personal questions, but you *will* be taught the facts about sex and your body.

Since 1994, it has been a legal requirement that all secondary schools should provide sex education.

Under the National Curriculum for Science, all 11 to 14 year olds have to be taught about the following:

- Sexually-transmitted infections, including the HIV virus and AIDS.
- The biological functions of your sexual organs. For instance, the functions of cells, ova, and sperm.
- Physical and emotional changes during puberty.
- Human reproductive systems, including the menstrual cycle and fertilisation.

- The development of a foetus in the uterus and the role of the placenta.
- Contraception.

How you'll be taught the above depends on your school and your teachers.

The Government also recommends the following should be included in school sex education:

- To have some understanding of the physical, emotional and social changes that take place at puberty.
- To know that there are many different patterns of friendship; and be able to talk about friends with adults.

- To understand the meaning of friendship and loyalty and begin to develop skills needed to form relationships.

Other places to go for sex education and information

1 **Your mum, dad or legal guardian** are the best people to ask for information about sex. Sadly, some parents are too embarrassed to bring up the subject and may do anything not to discuss it. If this is the case, try and encourage your parents/ guardian to talk, by bringing home a book or leaflet and asking them to explain things to you. If this doesn't work then ask them to point you in the right direction for help.

2 **A friend's parent, an older sister, brother or relative** can sometimes be easier to talk to, especially if your parents are embarrassed, if you don't get on with them or if they disagree with sex education.

3 **The library** is a good source for books and leaflets. Look in the Health section.

4 **Teen magazines** are usually a reliable source of information when it comes to sex, but don't make these your only source.

5 **Your doctor and practice nurse** at your local surgery. Your doctor has to follow confidential guidelines when it comes to the doctor/ patient relationship. This means you can go and talk to him or her and they can't tell your parents.

6 **Your local Family Planning or Brook Advisory Clinic.** They will answer any questions you have and/or give you some leaflets to look through.

Where not to get sex education

1 **Friends** may mean well, but they often get it wrong. Listening to friends is the quickest route to being misled.

2 **Older magazines.** You're likely to find lots of essentially correct information in women's and men's magazines, but these are directed at more sexually-experienced adults, so they won't be very helpful for someone just beginning to find out about sex.

3 **Porn magazines** are a waste of time on the
   information front. These magazines are aimed at
   men and are not a reliable source of information.

4 **Films and TV**. Unless you happen to be watching
   a documentary, don't bother to listen to any
   information given out in films and dramas. Despite
   what you see and hear, sex on screen is fictional,
   not real.

As good as some school sex education is, some areas are often left out, such as virginity and masturbation. There are many reasons why these aren't discussed, such as lack of time or a teacher's embarrassment, for example. The problem is, it's usually these very areas that cause teenagers most anxiety and worry. They are also the areas where you're most likely to find yourself weighed down by other people's views, making it hard to find your own way.

Virginity

"I'm a virgin and I hate it. I'm desperate to have sex."

Lisa (14)

"I once told my mates I was still a virgin and they've taken the mickey out of me ever since. They say I'm a sissy or make out girls don't fancy me. The thing is, I know for sure that at least two of them are as well."

Mark (14)

"I lost my virginity when I was 14. I feel like a slag when I think about that."

Hanna (16)

"I'm staying a virgin because my mum says men like you better that way."

Josie (12)

The dictionary definition of a virgin is *a person who has had no sexual intercourse*. Contrary to popular belief, virginity is not a 'sign' of anything. It doesn't mean you're a sexual loser who no-one wants, or some kind of prized possession with a special gift to give away.

The simple fact is, virginity, or a lack of it, doesn't reflect on your personality, even though there are idiots out there who will condemn you if you are and condemn you if you're not.

Always remember, if you are a virgin, that's great, and if you're not (and you're using contraception), that's okay too.

What's important is not to let other people's views – friends, girlfriends, boyfriends, parents or the media – make your mind up for you.

If you look at the papers you might think that every teenager in Britain is having sex, but research shows that four out of five women and three out of four men do not have sex before they are 16, so don't worry if you're still a virgin. It's perfectly normal.

The age of consent and virginity

The age of consent is 16 years old, which means that by law it is illegal for any male to have sex with a girl who is under 16 (17 in Northern Ireland). The age of consent is by no means a marker for losing your virginity. All it is is a legal device to protect young girls. Being 16 and having sex are unrelated. You have a right to say no, whatever your age.

Tips on how to deal with the question of virginity

- It's no-one's business but you're own whether you've had sex or not. If someone asks if you're a virgin, tell them to mind their own business.
- There's nothing humiliating about being a virgin, all it means is that you don't want to have sex yet.
- A man can't tell if you're a virgin. The hymen (piece of skin covering the entrance to the vagina), long believed to be "the sign" of virginity, can, and does, break very easily, so it's no guideline to whether or not a woman has had sex before.
- When it comes to sex, never pretend to be something you're not. Saying you're a virgin to get a guy or girl to like you, or making out you're not so he or she won't think less of you, is a waste of time. What's more, it can lead to all kinds of misunderstandings and problems.
- You're not a 'slut' or a 'stud' if you do have sex.

Masturbation

"I'm a bit confused about what masturbation is. Some of the boys in class asked about it and our teacher refused to discuss it."

Tina (13)

Masturbation means giving yourself sexual pleasure by touching your sexual organs. It doesn't make you blind, infertile, bad, or ruin your future sex life. Some people feel it's disgusting because they view masturbation as selfish or feel that the sexual organs should not be touched. Others say it's only for people who are single. However, the majority of the population masturbate in some form or another and it's not bad for you in any way. Masturbation is a perfectly normal and natural way to learn about your body. Boys masturbate by rubbing their penis, while girls usually masturbate by rubbing their clitoris in any way they find pleasurable.

Remember:

- Don't let anyone make you feel bad about masturbating. Most people do it, or have done it, even if they don't admit to it.
- Masturbating won't make you blind, put you off sex, make you sex mad, or ruin your chances of having a fulfilling sexual relationship with someone else.
- If you don't fancy it, don't do it. Masturbation is a personal, not a compulsory, issue.
- Always treat your sexual organs with care. They are extremely sensitive and delicate.

CHAPTER THREE

Love and relationships

What is love?

"It's being happy all the time." Liza (12)

"It's having a boyfriend to go out with." Ellie (13)

"It's when you like someone so much you can't stop thinking about them." Carl (14)

"Love happens when you go out with someone for a long time." Lizzie (11)

"My mum says love is over-rated." Paul (14)

"Love is listening to soppy love songs and buying those corny cards for each other." Jill (13)

Do you agree with any of the above? Or does being in love conjure up different images for you? Maybe you think of long-stemmed red roses, moonlight, and candlelit dinners. Maybe the very thought of love just makes you want to throw-up – or perhaps it makes you sad because you desperately want to be in love and haven't found someone special yet.

Love is actually all of these things and more. It's a complicated emotion that everyone (even those who deny it) wants to experience. If you and your friends have a different idea of what it means to be in love, don't worry. No-one is right and no-one is wrong. Love means something different to everyone, and it's not always as simple as Valentine's Day cards and flowers.

Sometimes it can feel like there's something wrong with us if no-one is in love with us. In an ideal world we'd see that being single doesn't mean we are defective in any way, but when everyone else seems to be happily in love we can sometimes feel pressurised into settling for just anyone for the sake of having a boyfriend or girlfriend. The fact is, unless you meet someone you really like, there is no reason to have a relationship.

Crushes

"I'm in love with a famous actor. I watch his films all the time and can't wait for the day I'm old enough to go and see him. My friends say I'm a fool to waste my time on someone who is probably a fake, but they don't know him the way I do. They don't realise how well-suited we are and how happy we could make each other."

Philippa (14)

"I've been in love with a pop star for two years. My friends and family say I am obsessed with him and I suppose they are right. What's the point in going out with boys I know, when all I want is him?"

Dion (13)

"Paul is my brother's best friend. He's 21 and the nicest guy I've ever met. He treats me like an adult, not a baby, and that's why I love him. The problem is, loving him makes me really sad, too, because I know we'll never get to go out because he's engaged to a girl his age. When I think of that I feel like crying."

Sharon (12)

Often most of us first experience love through a crush. This is when you get strong feelings for someone you don't really know. Some people think crushes are dangerous, or sad, or a road to unhappiness and misery. The fact is, having a crush is pretty normal and 90% of the population experience them at some point in their lives.

Crushes are just a safe way of learning how to deal with love, without having to actually go through a relationship. Some girls and boys can go through as many as ten crushes before they actually decide they want a real boyfriend or girlfriend. If you're someone who has crush after crush, don't worry; there's nothing wrong with you. Maybe you're just not ready to dive in and try the real thing, or perhaps you just haven't met the right person for you yet.

Serial crushes are only a problem if (1) – they stop you from giving the real people in your life a chance, and (2) – your crush is driving you to tears. If you're unhappy all the time, the chances are you think you're being cheated out of a relationship with your crush. If this is happening to you, you need to reassess the situation. After all, feeling genuine misery when you think about your crush means you've let your crush get out of control. Bring it back down to earth by limiting the amount of time you think about the person you fancy. This means setting aside time in the day to talk and think about him or her.

Painful as it is to admit, a crush on someone is mainly based on what the person looks like, what you've read or heard about them, and how you imagine them to be, not what you actually know. Most of us tend to heap all our biggest desires and needs on a crush, imagining they are the key to our happiness. The truth is, real love can only happen when you truly know someone. This is why dismissing the people you *do* know for imaginary love affairs is not a great idea. Real boys and girls may have faults, do stupid things, and act in irritating ways, but the benefits of a real boyfriend or girlfriend far outweigh these. Real boyfriends and girlfriends can make you laugh, share things with you and get intimate with you, which makes them a hundred times better than a crush.

Same-sex crushes

"I think I'm gay and I don't know what to do. I fancy my teacher but I feel too afraid to say anything."

Tim (15)

"I worry that I might be gay. I kissed a girl in the year above last year when I was on a school trip. No-one knows and I really regret it. What if someone finds out?"

Becky (13)

"We're all worried about a friend of ours. She is obsessed with this female actress and talks about her all the time. It's like she's in love with her. Do you think she might be a lesbian?"

Paula and Terri (14)

The fear that you might be gay is one of the most common fears of the teenage years. It may help to realise that although most of us end up with a definite preference, very few people are 100% heterosexual (straight) or homosexual (gay). This doesn't mean the majority of us have relationships with both sexes but it does mean most of us are capable of feeling some kind of attraction to members of both sexes.

This is why some people go through a period where they fancy a good friend or a famous person of the same sex. This isn't a sign of being gay, it's just a way of admitting you find a number of different characteristics and looks attractive.

No-one knows why some people are gay and others aren't. Ignore the stupid people who suggest that being friends with gay men or lesbian women can make you gay. Nothing can turn you gay; not books, films or your friends. Being gay is something that is a part of you; like your arm or your eye colour. Once you realise this, you'll see why homophobic people (people who dislike gays) are so ignorant. Lots of people have crushes on people of the same sex as they go through puberty – this doesn't mean that they are all gay. Puberty is a time of change, growth and experimentation. Don't label yourself before you know for sure what you want.

None of us can help who we fall in love with. If you *are* worried about your sexuality, don't just lock up all your true feelings and try to be something you're not. If you can't face telling anyone you know, there are a number of organisations who can and will help. They won't persuade you you're gay, straight or anything else for that matter. They'll just help you to come to terms with your mixed feelings.

Remember:

- Finding people of the same sex as yourself attractive means as little or as much as you want it to.
- As long as you're honest to yourself you don't owe anyone an explanation.

Relationships

"With all this talk about sex and what you should and shouldn't do, no-one ever talks about the obvious – how to get a boyfriend."

Donna (12)

Statistically your chances of getting a boyfriend or girlfriend are extremely high, but just because a girl or boy in your class has already gone out with lots of people and you haven't, it doesn't mean you're a loser. Some people spend the whole of their teens going from relationship to relationship while others find themselves single until they're in their twenties. I know at least two girls who didn't get their first boyfriend until they were 19, but have been dating ever since.

When it comes to love there are no hard and fast rules. Some people get lucky the first time, others have to kiss a load of toads before they meet the right person! If you're desperate for a boyfriend or girlfriend then you need to ask yourself why. Are you hoping that they will solve all the problems in your life? Do you think having a boyfriend or girlfriend will make you less lonely? More attractive? Or more acceptable to your friends? If any of these are your reasons then you need to think again.

Bad reasons for wanting a boyfriend or girlfriend:

1 You're bored.
2 You want to have sex.
3 Your friends have all got one.
4 You feel like a loser without one.
5 You're sick of having no stories to tell your friends.

6 It will make you feel attractive.
7 It will give you something to show off about.
8 Your parents want you to have one.

Good reasons for wanting a boyfriend or girlfriend:

1 You've met someone you like.
2 You've heard it's fun to go out with someone.
3 You want to experience being in love.

How to get – and keep – a boyfriend or girlfriend:

1 Be yourself.
2 Have a good social life of your own.
3 Have your own interests.
4 Don't be hung up on going out with someone.
5 Don't rush things. Make friends before you even try to go out with them.
6 Be interested in them as a person.
7 Treat them the way you'd treat your friends.
8 Make the first move when you meet a boy or girl you like.
9 Don't take them for granted.

Relationships are difficult and tricky things to get to grips with. They take a lot of effort and honesty. If you really like someone, you won't mind working things through with them. If you don't, then it's likely you'll run for cover the second trouble comes along. If you choose to do this, don't worry, it's likely they just weren't the right person for you. If you do stick around, take things day by day and don't rush into anything.

Dating

Getting a boyfriend or girlfriend is easy compared with learning to deal with dating someone. It may seem a simple thing, but juggling a relationship with your friendships, schoolwork and parents takes hard work and perseverance.

"I was terrible the first time I started seeing someone. I ignored all my friends, and, when I did see them, all I'd do was talk about him all the time. I refused to tell my parents what was going on and got in trouble at school. All I could think about was him, so when I was dumped, I felt like the world had ended."

Jeannie (14)

"I think going out with someone is hard. Your friends get jealous, your parents hassle you and everyone thinks you are having sex when you're not."

Louise (13)

The key to dealing with dating is to introduce your boyfriend or girlfriend to your friends and family. If they know him or her, they won't see them as a threat. And try not to talk about them all the time! In your eyes, your boyfriend or girlfriend may be the most interesting thing in the world, but they won't be to your family and friends.

When you are together, relax. This means, stop worrying about doing stuff wrong, or what he or she is thinking. No-one, least of all someone who likes you, expects you to be perfect. Embarrassing things happen to everyone and fumbling the first kiss or saying the wrong thing can easily be rectified with a quick apology or another try. As for worrying about the future, this is a waste of time because it means you're ignoring the present. You're supposed to enjoy your dates, not become anxiety-ridden about whether or not there'll be a next one!

Being gay

"I'm gay but my real problem is my dad. He's really anti-gay, and I know he'd chuck me out if I told him that I fancied boys. I can't live a lie forever, so what do I do?"

Tom (16)

"I know I'm gay. I keep trying to tell people but they say it's just a phase and I'll grow out of it. Others say, how can you know yet? But my friends know they fancy boys, so I know I fancy girls."

Alison (15)

Some people know from an early age that they're gay. However, it can be difficult to discuss this with other people as they might try to dismiss your views, not always because they're homophobic, but also because they don't believe you should label your sexuality when you're still a teenager. If you are in this situation, it can really help to talk to someone in a similar position so you can see you're not alone. The Lesbian and Gay Switchboard (see Resources) runs a 24 hour service for anyone who needs to talk.

However, don't rush into coming out (telling people you're gay) until you have come to terms with your feelings. Sexual identity is a personal thing. Take your time and do it when you feel happier about who you are. Remember, you have nothing to feel 'bad' about. Being gay is part of who you are.

Coming out

Coming out is not easy, but it's easier than spending your whole life pretending to be something you're not. Of course there are going to be people who don't understand, but you should never let other people's prejudices stop you from being honest about yourself. After all, being gay isn't an illness, it's an alternative to being straight.

If you're thinking of coming out, you may find it helpful to talk to someone first. If your friends and family react badly, give them time – for some people it has more to do with lost expectations than the fact that you're gay. After all, coming out doesn't mean you've suddenly changed.

Remember:

• Discovering you're gay isn't the end of the world. The image of a gay man or woman being all alone is a false one. Just like heterosexuals, the majority of gay people have partners to share their lives with. If you feel isolated, try talking to someone in a similar situation – the Lesbian and Gay Switchboard will be able to help.

Is this love?

"I get really confused by girls. You ask them out, you have a good time together and then all of a sudden they start getting serious and talking about being in love with you. Then they get angry when you won't say it to them."

Neil (14)

"I've been seeing Dave for a month and I really like him. The problem is he keeps saying he loves me and expects me to say it back. He's been on about it since we started seeing each other and I kind of feel he doesn't really know what it is. It's like he thinks this is what couples say to each other."

Kelly (13)

Dating someone and falling in love don't necessarily go hand in hand. Sometimes, you can really, really like someone, like Kelly, but not be in love with them. When this happens it can be hard, especially if they keep saying 'I love you', and you don't feel like saying it back. If this is happening to you, don't worry. Love takes time to develop and when you feel ready to say it, you will. Until then don't feel guilty or mean. It's better to be honest about your feelings than lie to save someone else's. As for people who say 'I love you' from the beginning of a relationship, the chances are they are just saying it because they think it's what's expected of them.

"I feel totally confused. I think I love Paul, but it's not like how I feel about my mum or my dog. Sometimes, I can't imagine life without him, then other times he really annoys me and makes me mad."

Anne (13)

"I really like my girlfriend, sometimes I even think I love her, but I've never told her because it makes me feel embarrassed."

Craig (14)

The most perplexing thing about going out with someone is working out how you really feel about them. The question of whether or not we're really in love is the dilemma most of us get caught up in. We worry that we don't love the person we're with enough, or we worry that we love them too much. We sometimes even worry that secretly we don't love them at all.

Below are just some of the ways people say they can tell when they're in love.

- "He's the first thing I think of in the morning, and the last thing I think of at night."
- "You want to do nice things for them all the time."
- "You worry that they'll get hurt."
- "You think nothing of putting them first."
- "You miss them when you're not with them."
- "Silly things remind you of them."
- "You just know."

What's important to remember is that being in love with someone doesn't mean that suddenly you'll never get mad, angry or irritated with them again. Being in love also doesn't mean that all your problems will disappear overnight and you'll be happy all the time. If you think this is what love is, you're going to be sorely disappointed.

CHAPTER FOUR

Thinking about sex

Feeling under pressure

"I love my boyfriend a lot. More than anyone I've ever met. The problem is I don't think I'm ready for sex, but he won't let it go. He says if I loved him I'd do it. Sometimes, I think maybe he's right."

Lara (13)

"My girlfriend has got it into her head that couples going steady have to do it. I don't feel we know each other well enough yet but she's taking it as a sign that I don't love her."

Sam (15)

You don't need me to tell you that sex isn't the next step after kissing. It isn't even the next step after touching and exploring. It's only the next step if you want it to be. There's nothing wrong with not wanting to have sex, nor is there anything slutty about having sex. Sex is something that lots of people have an opinion on: there are people who will tell you it's a bad idea and you should keep away – parents, politicians, and some doctors, for example – and people who will try and encourage you to do it – like boyfriends and friends. Somewhere amongst all of this you have to find your own voice and decide what's right for you. The basic rule is, if someone is putting you under pressure to have sex, they are only thinking about themselves, and not you.

Sex and the law

You already know the age of consent refers to the legal age by which a girl can give her consent to have sex. But did you know it is actually an offence for any male to have sex with a girl who is under 16 years of age? If caught, a boy who is over 17, can get two years in prison. If he is under 17 he will usually get a warning. In most cases the police don't prosecute, but that's usually after a lot of questioning and hassle.

The age of consent actually only refers to girls, although women who have sex with boys who are under 16 can be charged with indecent assault. The age of consent for male homosexuals is 16. There is no age of consent regarding two women having sex together.

With all this talk about the law, it's easy to start believing the age of consent is a marker, or a guide to losing your virginity. This is a load of rubbish. It's a legal guideline and that's all. Having sex is about when you're ready, and for most people this happens well after the age of 16.

Feeling ready for sex

How do you know when you're ready to have sex? Some people say it's to do with age, others to do with how long you've been dating. Some people suggest "a person just knows", while others claim "people never know". The fact is, having sex means only one thing: taking responsibility for yourself – and this means the only person who can tell if you're ready is YOU. If you have any doubts, the truth is you're probably not ready. If this is the case, then wait. After all, what's all the rush?

When it's not right to have sex

- Your boyfriend says if you really loved him you'd have sex.
- Your best friend says it's no big deal.
- You think sex will make him love you more.
- You want a baby.
- You want to annoy your mum.
- You're curious.
- You think it's time you lost your virginity.
- You want something to talk about.
- You think sex will make you feel attractive and wanted.
- Your boyfriend says he'll leave if you don't do it.
- You think you're too old to be a virgin.

When it's okay to have sex

- You care about each other and you've discussed wanting to have sex.
- You trust each other.
- You've talked about contraception and visited your doctor or a clinic or chemist to get contraception.
- You've weighed up all the pros and cons.

How to say no to sex

Saying no to sex can be hard, especially when you really care about someone. However, it *is* possible to say no and still carry on seeing someone. All it takes is the right words. Of course, finding the right words can be tough when you feel under pressure, or scared that you're going to lose someone.

Below are a few ways to say no:

- **"I'm just not ready to go all the way."**
  This is a good one, because it's not an apology (after all if you're not ready, you're not ready, so why apologise) and it explains why you don't want to have sex.

- **"We can talk about this but I still don't want to have sex."**
  Sometimes, people think you need to be persuaded into having sex and so they'll try to reason with you. This is why you need to be specific from the beginning that while you're happy to talk about your reasons this isn't an open invitation to be talked into something.

- **"It's too soon."**
  Some people have sex after being together for two weeks, other people can wait for two years or more before they do it. Some people are ready at 16, others earlier, others later. The fact is, there is no hard and fast rule to being ready for sex. If you think it's too soon, then it is too soon.

- **"We don't know each other well enough."**
  You can be seeing someone for a few months and still feel you don't know them well enough to have sex. Going out, having fun and being together doesn't necessarily equal intimacy and trust.
  If you feel at all unsure about someone, then wait until you're more sure.

- **"It's too scary."**
  Being scared of having sex is pretty common – and not just from the what to do and what happens next angle. Lots of people worry about catching a sexual disease or getting pregnant, and even using a condom doesn't put their mind at rest.

If the thought of having sex worries you and fills you with fear, then say so. Having sex when you feel like this is disastrous and isn't likely to be a pleasant experience.

- **"I don't want to have sex but I really like you and want to see you."**
There's nothing like saying the obvious to get your message across. Most people are pretty okay with a girlfriend or boyfriend who says no, as long as they are clear that it's the sex you're rejecting, not them.

Be direct about why you're saying no and they won't feel hurt or unloved. Shrug it off and refuse to discuss it and they'll imagine the worst.

Even if you try all of the above, you're still bound to come across people who just won't take no for an answer. Maybe they'll try one of the following lines on you:

"But it's bad for me to want sex and not to do it."

"If you loved me you would."

"I'll leave you if you don't."

"My last girlfriend/boyfriend did."

"I didn't realise I was dating a baby."

"What's the matter – are you scared?"

"What's the big deal?"

"Matt was my first boyfriend and he knew I was inexperienced when it came to relationships, so he took advantage of that. He tried to pressurise me into having sex. Whenever I said no, he'd make out I was being a baby. Luckily, I knew I was in the right and dumped him."

Susie (13)

"I think Lucy went out with me because she heard I'd had sex with my last girlfriend. For some reason she was desperate to have sex with me and kept trying to pressurise me into it. When I said no, she told all her friends I was gay."

Stephen (15)

Boyfriends or girlfriends who won't wait until you're ready are only looking out for themselves. Don't be fooled, if they are not ready to wait, they are not right for you.

WARNING: Having sex for the wrong reasons or being bullied into it, means it's likely to be a miserable experience. If you're not happy about it, don't do it.

Sex myths

- **All boys want sex – NOT TRUE!**
  This is a common myth based on the idea that boys have higher sex drives than girls. While there are some boys whose aim in life is to bed as many girls as possible, they are in the minority. The majority of boys are just as scared about sex, relationships and the opposite sex as girls are.

- **Everybody's doing it – NOT TRUE!**
Everybody's talking about it, but not everybody's doing it. If you are surrounded by friends who boast about having sex, take what they say with a pinch of salt. For a start, sex isn't something to show off about. It's a private thing between two people. Girls and boys who feel the need to tell all to everyone are usually trying to hide something.

- **Having sex means you are grown-up – NOT TRUE!**
Sex doesn't have anything to do with being grown-up, mature or adult. In fact, lots of adults make terrible mistakes when it comes to sex. They rush into things, and live to regret it in the same way that you and I might do. Being older doesn't mean you're wiser, in the same way that doing adult things doesn't make you an adult.

- **Sex strengthens a relationship – NOT TRUE!**
Sex only strengthens a relationship that's already strong. That means a relationship where you know and care about each other, where you've taken time to get to know each other, where you've discussed things, and taken the right precautions. If you haven't done these things, sex will only weaken your relationship.

- **Sex is difficult – NOT TRUE!**
It's not difficult to actually have sex. The physical act is fairly straightforward, it's the after-effects that are difficult. If you've had sex for the wrong reasons, the morning after can be a nightmare.

Protecting yourself emotionally

Sex can mean as much or as little as you want it to. However, if you don't think about what you're doing, plan things or use contraception, you're heading for disaster.

Why are you doing it?

It's good to consider why you're having sex before you go ahead and do it. Sometimes, looking at these reasons can safeguard you from getting hurt or used. You're looking for trouble if you have sex for any of these reasons:

- Your boyfriend or girlfriend say they'll leave you if you don't.
- You want to be grown up.
- You've heard it's great.
- Your friends are persuading you to do it.

- You're 16.
- You know your boyfriend or girlfriend had sex in their last relationship.
- You feel you should.

Can your relationship handle the pressure of having sex?

How well do you know the person you're going to have sex with? Will your relationship be able to stand up to the pressures of a sex life? You should be able to answer yes to all of the following before you have sex.

1 Have you talked about contraception?
2 Have you discussed what will happen after you've had sex?
3 Have you talked about your worries and fears?
4 Do you know what you'd do if you got pregnant?
5 If he or she is not a virgin, have they always practised safe sex (i.e. used a condom to protect against sexually-transmitted infections)?
6 Does your boyfriend or girlfriend have your best interests at heart?

If you're going to have sex, do yourself a favour: plan things out properly. For your first time you don't want to have to rush things because you're worried someone will walk in on you. If you're both sure this is what you want, you owe it to yourselves to plan things out, so it is as relaxing an experience as possible.

Protecting yourself physically

Contraception and safe sex

So, you've decided that you are ready to have sex, but the question of contraception should be on your lips before you do anything. In 1985, the House of Lords established the current legal position regarding teenagers and medical treatment in the UK. They said that: "People under 16, who are able to fully understand what is proposed and its implications, are competent to consent to medical treatment regardless of age."

This means it's up to your doctor to decide whether or not you're mature enough to receive contraception.

They'll decide this based upon your ability to understand what is being offered to you and your reasons behind wanting it.

While most doctors think if you're mature enough to be asking for contraception, you're mature enough to be given it, there are some who might turn you down. However, even if your doctor does say no, he or she must keep your request confidential and you can go to another doctor or clinic. You can also go and buy condoms from any chemist as it is not illegal to buy contraceptives when you're under sixteen.

Warning:
Don't be fooled into thinking you can side-step contraception. Last year 85,000 girls aged 14 –19 got pregnant. By not using contraception you not only leave yourself open to pregnancy but also to AIDS and several sexually-transmitted infections. It is important to practise safe sex at all times. Safe sex means protecting yourself from the risk of infection and disease. Using a condom will also guard against pregnancy (see Chapter Seven for more information).

Types of contraception

The condom

Description: Looks like a latex rubber balloon, but comes rolled in a packet.

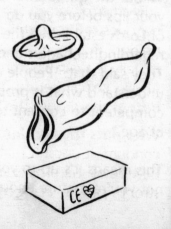

Works by: Preventing sperm entering the vagina by catching it in the end of the condom. They are designed to be put over an erect penis before sex, they come in one size and, despite stories of them ripping, are very strong. Make sure the condoms you use have the EU (European Union) symbol and the British Kitemark (a small triangle) on the packet, as this means they have been tested for durability.

How to use: Open the packet carefully, squeeze the closed end (it looks like a nipple) and roll down over the erect penis before intercourse. After sex, hold the condom firmly in place so it doesn't slip off as the penis goes limp, then remove carefully and throw away.

Many boys and some girls feel wearing a condom lessens their sexual pleasure. If you feel this is a problem, try extra-sensitive condoms which are made of very fine rubber and should improve sensation. If you're worried about fitting into a condom, don't – one size fits all. In fact, they can stretch up to half a metre in length and over 40cm in width!

Warning: Never re-use a condom or use Vaseline (or any other oil-based lubricant) near it. Vaseline and heat destroy condoms and make them prone to ripping. If extra lubrication or moisture is needed, KY Jelly is available from chemists for this purpose. Always check the use-by date and don't store near heat as this erodes the latex.

Who puts the condom on: As long as you use a condom, it doesn't matter who puts it on. However, beware of sharp nails and jewellery. Condoms, while strong, can be snagged pretty easily on sharp objects.

Where to get them: Chemists, supermarkets or free from clinics and your doctor.

How effective?: 97% if used properly

Major plus: The safest way to protect you from STIs and HIV.

The pill

Description: A small hormone pill that you swallow. This comes in packets of three months supply. Each packet has a separate strip of pills and each pill is labelled for a day of the week. One pill is taken every day.

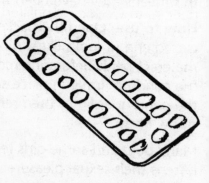

Works by: Either stopping an egg from being released from the ovary or by stopping a fertilised egg from being implanted in the uterus.

How to use: Usually you take one a day for three weeks, stop for a week's break when you will have a period and then start a new pack. However, there are different types of pill and instructions may vary. Always read the leaflet included in the pack.

Warning: The pill won't protect you from STIs or HIV.

Where to get it: Only available on prescription from your doctor or a clinic.

How effective?: 99% if used properly

Major plus: It doesn't interfere with sex and can relieve painful periods.

Not recommended for teenagers

The rhythm method

This works on the principal that there are certain days within your cycle when you can have sex without getting pregnant. It's not suitable for young people because you need to have extremely regular periods to work out your fertile and infertile days. It also means you have to plan sex. On top of all this, this method does not protect you from HIV and STIs (sexually-transmitted infections).

Persona

This is a new machine available from Boots, designed to work as a computerised rhythm method. Not recommended for all of the above reasons, plus it's expensive and best suited for older women in long-term relationships.

Warning: With both these forms of the rhythm method, you must avoid sex (or use a condom) on the days deemed 'dangerous' i.e. days you are most likely to get pregnant.

IUD (Intra-Uterine Device)

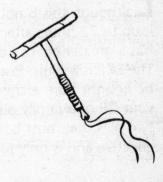

Also known as 'the coil'. This is a small plastic and copper device in the shape of an anchor, which is placed in the uterus. It stops fertilised eggs from settling in the uterus by irritating the uterus lining.

It offers no protection against HIV or STIs and can cause cramps and bleeding. It's usually only given to older women, but can be used as an emergency form of contraception and inserted up to five days after having unprotected sex. See your doctor or local Family Planning clinic for details.

Diaphragm

Also known as 'the cap'. This looks like a thin rubber dome. It is placed inside the vagina before sex and has to be kept in for up to six hours after sex. It's used with spermicide cream, which creates a sperm-killing barrier and increases protection. The cream is spread over the 'cap' before insertion. A diaphragm needs a lot of planning and forethought, including fitting by a doctor in the first instance.

Not recommended as forms of contraception

Emergency Contraceptive Pill

ECP is also known as the morning after pill, although this is not strictly correct as you can take it up to 72 hours after unprotected sex. However, it has a greater chance of working the faster you take it. The ECP is a high dose contraceptive pill and can now be bought from a chemist or be prescribed free by your GP or a family planning clinic. EPC is made up of two pills that must be taken 12 hours apart. It is 96% effective and is only for emergencies, not regular use.

Withdrawal

Not a reliable form of contraception. Withdrawal is when a boy removes his penis from a girl's vagina before he ejaculates. It's a useless method because sperm can and does leak out before ejaculation. It's impossible to control this – so don't believe any boy who says they can stop it happening.

Douching

This is the name given to washing out the vagina after sex. It doesn't work and may even increase the chances of pregnancy and vaginal infections.

Remember:

1 You can get pregnant the first time you have sex.
2 You can't get pregnant through oral sex or kissing.
3 Sex standing up doesn't stop you getting pregnant.
4 Having sex during your period is not a method of contraception.
5 You can't re-use a condom.
6 If you forget to take your pill, taking two pills the next day won't help.
7 You can't borrow someone else's pills.
8 Spermicide cream on its own is not a form of contraception.

CHAPTER FIVE

Having sex

What actually happens

Believe it or not, the mechanics of sex are fairly simple. However, there is a lot of confusion about the different terms and stages. These are explained below.

Step one: French kissing and getting intimate

Most couples start their relationship with kissing, but there is one kind of kiss in particular that worries people – the French kiss.

French kissing is open-mouthed kissing. Instead of kissing someone on the lips, both partners open their mouths slightly and use their tongues to explore each other's mouths. The key to this is being relaxed and easy about it. It's a bit awkward at first, but if it goes wrong, just try again. Some people think French kissing sounds like the most disgusting thing in the world, it really isn't, but if someone is unhappy about

French kissing, they shouldn't do it. After all, French kissing is an intimate form of kissing and shouldn't be attempted if one partner isn't into it.

Kissing and feeling or exploring each other's bodies through clothes, is a way of starting to get to know each other more intimately before considering a further step.

Step two – foreplay

Foreplay, also known as 'heavy petting', is sexual activity that happens before intercourse, although it doesn't always lead to penetration.

It usually begins with couples kissing, touching, stroking and feeling each other to the point where they feel ready for intercourse or orgasm. Foreplay can involve just about anything, from oral sex to simple hugging, but it is entirely up to the couple involved what it includes – for example, one person may not want to do something their partner suggests, and it is up to them to say so. During foreplay, couples usually explore each other's bodies with their hands and mouths. It's easy to concentrate on the breasts and genital areas but the body has other erogenous zones (areas that give rise to sexual excitement) that can also add to sexual pleasure. These usually vary from person to person, but include areas like the nape of the neck, the inner thighs and the spine. Foreplay is an excellent way to get to know each other's bodies and also to find out what makes each partner feel good. In order to find out what works, couples experiment and talk about what they like. If one partner is too embarrassed to say out loud what they want, they can try leading their partner in the right direction with their hands. Basically, the best rule of thumb for foreplay is to do what makes each person feel comfortable. Not things that are 'expected' or demanded by others.

Step three – moving nearer to sexual intercourse

Men and women get sexually aroused in different ways. Male arousal is more obvious because men get an erection. This is when the penis fills with blood and goes from being limp to being stiff and upright. It will also feel hot and become darker in colour. It's at this point that a condom should be rolled on to the penis, as a few drops of semen can come out even before ejaculation. As a woman becomes aroused, her body will become more sensitive to the touch and her vagina will begin to feel moist and lubricated in preparation for intercourse. The sexual organs and the breasts swell slightly and the skin becomes flushed.

Some people like to try oral sex at this stage, but others don't. There are other ways to stimulate each other without having to perform things one partner is unsure of. Many women like having their genital area stroked, especially the clitoris, which is extremely sensitive. This kind of stimulation often leads to female orgasm. Men too, like having their genital region touched and stroked, particularly the penis.

Step four — sexual intercourse

Usually this state of arousal carries on until neither person can wait any longer. It's at this point that sexual intercourse occurs. This is when a man puts his penis inside a woman's vagina. Sometimes it can be difficult to enter the vagina, and trying repeatedly can make the woman sore. Women can help out their boyfriends by guiding the penis into the vagina. Once the penis is inside the vagina, the man and woman move rhythmically together, thrusting their hips to increase contact until they reach orgasm and the man ejaculates.

An orgasm is the climax of sexual excitement. It follows a similar pattern for both girls and boys, although the feelings and sensations often differ, both from time to time and from person to person. At the peak of sexual excitement, the sex organs contract in a series of muscular spasms, followed by a feeling of release and pleasure as the muscles relax.

Boys have an obvious physical sign of orgasm which is ejaculation. When this happens a white substance called semen (also known as 'spunk' or 'cum') is released from the penis.

Very few women orgasm (climax) simply through sexual intercourse, because there aren't any nerve endings in the vagina. The majority of female orgasms occur from stimulation (rubbing, kissing and touching) around the clitoris and the entrance to the vagina, before, during and/or after intercourse. Some women take longer than others to have an orgasm, and not all women have an orgasm every time they have sex - everyone is different. As a woman gets to know her body and how it feels during foreplay and later during sex, she will be able to work out what helps her to orgasm and what doesn't.

Step five — after sex

After sex some people hold each other and kiss, some lie there and talk, others fall asleep. There are no rules, each person does what makes them comfortable.

Common concerns

Even when you've discussed every possible aspect of having sex and feel you are ready – when it gets to the actual physical act, it's still normal to be worried. So it's good to be aware of other problems that can occur. Here are some of the most common concerns people have about sex.

Erection problems

Many boys worry that when it actually comes to having sex, they won't be able to get an erection. Sadly, worry, anxiety and stress all make it worse. If a boy can't get an erection, it's not a sign that he doesn't fancy his partner or has changed his mind – it's much more likely that he's trying too hard. If his partner is understanding and tells him it doesn't matter, he'll be more likely to relax and eventually get an erection.

Painful sex

Sex can seem like a big thing and everyone gets the jitters even if they are 100% sure they want to do it. Sometimes this nervousness can cause a girl's vagina to go into spasm, which means that penetration (the penis entering the vagina) can be painful. Some girls find that they are too dry for entry and this can be painful too.

Panicking only makes things worse. Slowing things down and going back to kissing helps both partners to relax and feel more at ease. KY jelly (available without prescription from chemists) can also help, by lubricating the vagina (making it more slippery).

The hymen can also make sex painful. Lots of girls bleed when they have sex for the first time because the hymen breaks during penetration (the hymen breaking may produce a short, sharp pain). However, the hymen is broken very easily through sport or the use of tampons, so if there is no blood, it doesn't mean the girl isn't a virgin. The hymen is no indication of virginity at all.

Bad smells

Clean sex organs do have their own individual smells, usually a kind of musky odour. No-one's genital area is supposed to smell of roses. Some people find this musky smell very arousing, and as long as the genitals are clean, there is nothing to worry about.

Premature ejaculations

First-time sex can be a rushed, over-in-two-minutes affair, simply because when people are rushed, nervous or new to the whole thing, it's hard to keep control. Boys in particular may get excited far too quickly and come (ejaculate) before they've even had sex. When this happens a boy will lose his erection and won't be able to have sex. However, this isn't the end of the world and with practice and time, he'll learn to control his ejaculations.

Buying contraception

Couples who are mature enough to have sex, should be mature enough to approach the question of contraception together. This means both partners should go along to their doctor, Brook Clinic or Family Planning Clinic to get sorted.

"I'm still a virgin and my mum has warned me about all the risks of unprotected sex but I'd still feel cheap having a condom on me. I mean, what would the guy think if he saw me pull it out?"

Lisa (13)

Of course, there are still some guys who think it's up to the girl to get sorted and some girls who think it looks bad if a girl has contraception on her, but there's nothing wrong with being prepared or bringing up the subject of contraception. If contraception is an awkward issue between a couple, it probably means they aren't ready to have sex.

WAITING ROOM

Endless love?

Sex can last from two minutes to two hours or more. People often think of sex as being the actual act of putting the penis in the vagina, when it's much more than this. Sex includes kissing, cuddling and touching and this is why it can last longer than two hours. However, there are no hard and fast rules and no time limits to live up to.

When it's all over...

Ask around and you'll find a variety of different ways that people act after sex. For some men and women, sleep seems to be the most popular answer. This is the body's response to the physical strain of having sex. Some couples prefer cuddling and talking, others just want to get away as soon as possible. The best thing to do is talk about it and try and find a compromise which makes both partners feel comfortable.

 "When we started having sex it was always horrible afterwards because my boyfriend would rush to get away. I felt really used by him and we nearly broke up over it. Later I discovered his ex-girlfriend always used to ask him to leave after sex, so he thought this was the way all girls reacted."

Jane (17)

Experience vs. inexperience

Having one partner more experienced than the other can work for or against you. A more experienced partner may be more considerate and caring, helping to make the experience more pleasurable.

However, they may also be more demanding, putting pressure on their less-experienced partner to go further than they want.

The other negative side of sleeping with someone experienced is that there may be a certain amount of anxiety about what they expect.

> "When it came to sex I always felt like I had to live up to Tom's ex-girlfriend. She was older than me and I knew she'd slept with a few people. I felt that he was always comparing her to me."
>
> Tara (14)

A couple who are both virgins may feel more at ease with each other, simply because there will be fewer expectations about sex. However, previous partners (too many or too few), should not be an issue. Just because one partner has already lost their virginity doesn't make them a better or a worse person.

Stopping things once you've started

Anyone can say no to sex at any time, but it's important to be sensitive about it. In an ideal world all their worries should have been worked through before getting down to the nitty gritty.

However, if one partner changes their mind after saying yes, they should say so right away. Waiting until penetration is about to occur is unfair and won't win them any respect from their boyfriend or girlfriend.

Whether having sex once means having sex every time.

"After I had sex for the first time I felt under pressure to keep doing it every time we met. Then one day my boyfriend turned round and said 'do you mind if we just hang out and don't do it?' I was so relieved and surprised that he felt the same way as me."

Lucy (14)

Saying yes to sex is always a choice and saying yes once doesn't mean it's necessary to keep having sex all the time. Though it's hard to go back to holding hands after having sex, it can be done. If sex was a mistake, then it's best to say so. As long as it's clear it's the sex being rejected, not the person, things should work out fine.

First-time sex

Once they've had sex, some people are pleased, others regret it. Perhaps they have made a mistake and don't know what to do about it. Some worry that people will think they're a 'slut' or 'easy'. It can be tough having sex for the first time for a number of reasons. The main one is feeling alone and cut off from everyone else.

"After I had sex with Mark I felt really bad. Even though I'd been sure the day before, the following morning I felt like I'd done something wrong. I couldn't tell my mum because I knew she'd freak out. I couldn't tell my friends because I didn't want them to know and I couldn't talk to Paul because I didn't want to upset him. I felt totally alone and scared."

Sue (14)

"Before I lost my virginity everyone made out they were doing it too, afterwards I realised they'd all been lying and I was the only one who'd gone all the way."

Ben (15)

"I've had sex and I don't feel bad about it, though everyone wants me to say I do – I think just so they'll feel they're right and I'm wrong."

Fran (14)

Remember:

- Don't let anyone make you feel bad about losing your virginity. You made a decision and letting someone make you feel bad about it won't achieve anything.
- There is no such thing as a 'slag' or 'being easy'– these are sexist terms used by ignorant idiots and are best ignored.

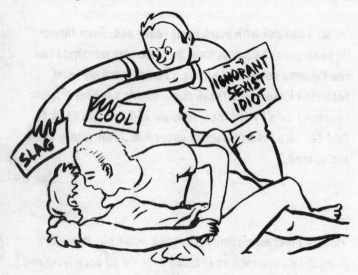

- The issues surrounding virginity and having sex are scary no matter whether you're male or female. We all worry about sex, no matter what we say.
- If you need to talk to someone, but can't confide in anyone you know, then contact Childline (see Resources). Talking through your worries with someone anonymous can be a welcome relief.
- Being bullied into having sex, or doing it for the wrong reasons will always lead to a miserable experience.

Many people are deeply disappointed by their first attempt at sex, which is partly because they have high expectations due to films, TV and other people's stories. Everyone, including experienced adults, knows that having sex with someone for the first time is not always mind-blowing. It takes time for most couples to get to know each other's bodies, wants and needs. Everyone feels inhibited and shy the first time they get naked with someone they care about. But with time it gets better and starts feeling more like making love.

Real—life experiences

"It was weird – a kind of good weird, but weird all the same."

Dan

"It's nothing like I expected. I thought it would be more romantic and it wasn't."

Jen

"It was over so fast, I wondered if we'd actually done it."

Paula

"I didn't expect much because my sister said it was painful and embarrassing, but I must have been lucky because it was really fun and sweet."

Janey

"I was terrified when I saw his erection. I thought 'no way is that going to fit in me' so I made him stop."

Anne

"He was so weird, he didn't say a word the whole time."

Jill

"I felt embarrassed lying there naked while she was getting undressed."

Mark

"He put my hand on his thing and I nearly died of shock."

Lisa

"I liked most of it, but when he was inside me it really hurt and I couldn't wait for it to stop."

Julie

"It was much better than I thought. In fact we did it twice."

James

"I did wonder what all the fuss was about. But now we've done it loads of times, it's got better and I can see what the big deal is."

Sam

CHAPTER SIX

Life after sex

What now?

"After we had sex I wasn't sure what was supposed to happen next. I stupidly thought my boyfriend and I would be closer but it turned out he avoided me for about a week. When I did see him again, he couldn't even look me in the eye and got his friend to tell me it was all over."

Jo (13)

"After the first time we had sex, I panicked. I kept worrying my boyfriend would want me to have sex all the time, so I made sure we were never alone. It took me ages to tell him I still fancied him but didn't want to have sex again."

Carla (16)

People who have just had sex for the first time may be anxious afterwards. Apart from the shall-we–shan't-we–try-it-again syndrome, there's the how-do-we-handle-things-now question to deal with. Sadly, there is no recommended after-sex instruction manual, because different options work for different people. Some people find talking about what happened afterwards can help ease any anxiety. This doesn't mean reliving every moment verbally. It does, however, mean being honest (but tactful) about what was good and what was bad.

Remember:

There is no minimum requirement to sex. Just because someone has sex on one occasion, doesn't mean they have to keep doing it, or, in fact, ever do it again. Some people feel once they've hit the sex stage, they can't go back to just kissing. This is rubbish.

A sign of a good relationship is being able to be close without having sex. If one partner expects sex all the time, it's up to the other to set up some boundaries, thinking about what they want and why. If one partner decides sex was all a big mistake, they don't have to do it again.

On the other hand, if both partners are happy having sex on a regular basis, that's fine, as long as contraception is used and arrangements have been made to look after their sexual health (see pages 100–1). What 'on a regular basis' means is up to them. Ignore national statistics of couples having sex X amount of times a week, and friends who tell you they are at it all the time. Apart from statistics being unreliable and friends exaggerating, sex is a personal issue and not something to be competitive over.

After-sex worries

"Sex was terrible. It hurt (and not because of my hymen) and wasn't enjoyable at all. What went wrong?"

Steph

First time sex can be painful and joyless for the following reasons:

- Not taking things gently and slowly.
- Not showing caring and loving behaviour.
- Choosing uncomfortable positions to have sex in.
- Ignoring foreplay.
- Rushing sex for fear of being discovered.
- Having sex with someone you don't trust.
- Having sex with someone you don't know.
- Having sex with someone who only cares about their own satisfaction.

"Am I frigid? Last night I was ready to have sex with my boyfriend, but when we got down to it, I just froze. I felt sick when he touched me and couldn't even kiss him."

Laura

"We kissed and petted for a while and nothing happened. I felt so ashamed, it was like I'd let her down. I just got dressed and left before she could say anything."

Tom

Sometimes people think they're ready for sex but when it comes down to it, they're not. When this happens, girls are likely to tense up and boys find they can't get, or keep, an erection. This can be pretty distressing, upsetting and confusing. However, don't be fooled into thinking it's a sign of being frigid or impotent. It's just a sign that they're not yet ready to have sex.

"Will my boyfriend think I'm cheap? I'm worried because I had sex with him to show him how much I loved him but now I feel like I've been too easy."

Fran

"I've had sex with one boy and now everyone says I am a slut. It was my ex-boyfriend who started this just because I said no to him. It's really unfair. He's slept with six girls and his friends think he's brilliant for it, so why am I getting so much hassle?"

Lena

Any boy who sleeps with a girl and then turns round and labels her 'easy', a 'slut', or 'cheap' deserves to be ditched on the spot.

Not only is name-calling a sign that he doesn't have his girlfriend's best interests at heart, but it's also a sign of stupidity and immaturity. After all, if he thinks she's cheap for having sex, what is he? Men or women who have these double standards should be ignored.

"My boyfriend and I had sex for the first time three days ago. Since then he's been acting weird with me. He doesn't call and when we meet up he pretends nothing happened."

Donna (15)

"I slept with Claire a week ago and she's ignored me ever since. I keep trying to think what went wrong and what she's mad at me about."

Tony (15)

Many people believe that when it comes to sex, boys are naturally at ease with it. The fact is, boys worry just as much as girls. If one person starts acting weird after sex, it's time to talk. Maybe they are embarrassed about being naked, or by the actual sexual act. Or perhaps they just don't know what to say. Talking is always the best solution.

It's pretty much a myth that boys want sex all the time and that if they fancy someone they can't wait to sleep with them.

Guys have a right to stay virgins too and a right to say no to sex without being labelled odd, weird or strange.

One-night stands

"I lost my virginity on a one-night stand. I pretend I don't mind, but I do. I really thought this boy liked me but he hasn't spoken to me since."

Paula

Reasons why one-night stands are a bad idea

- Meeting someone for the first time and having sex with them is dangerous for a number of reasons. One, they could be aggressive or violent. Two, sex is unlikely to be pleasurable because neither person knows or trusts the other. Three, not knowing how sexually active they are means putting yourself at risk of developing an STI, unless a condom is used.
- Being physically intimate with someone is not the same as being intimate with them. Beginning with sex means it's difficult to get back to the "So what's your name?" stage.

- Having sex to get a boyfriend is a mistake. Very few one night stands turn into relationships. If you fancy someone and want them to know you like them, tell them. It's easier, safer and a lot less hassle than having sex.
- Having a one night stand isn't the ego-boost it might seem – and may even leave both people feeling worse about themselves.

"I had sex when I was drunk. Now I'm worried we didn't use contraception and I can't remember what happened."

Sara

Drunken sex is the number one way people put themselves at risk from pregnancy and STIs. If this does happen and they suspect they had sex without a condom, the best thing to do is to visit the doctor or a clinic as soon as possible. The morning-after pill has to be taken within 72 hours of unprotected sex if a woman is to prevent pregnancy, and any infections should be treated straightaway.

Remember:

Using drink as a way to get courage is looking for trouble. Alcohol makes people feel braver but it actually lowers their inhibitions, making them more likely to do dangerous things without realising it.

Sexual health

"I know where to get contraception from but I'm confused about how to stay healthy. My friend says I've got to go and have internals and smears, but they sound so scary. Do I have to do this and where do I go?"

Charlotte

People who are mature enough to have sex, should also be wise enough to make sure they are looking after their sexual health. The hardest part of this is learning how to face a doctor and tell her or him what's wrong.

Some reasons to see the doctor:

- Women having regular sex need to have a smear test (to check the cells of the cervix).
- A strange, itchy or smelly discharge is a possible sign of infection.
- If periods stop – this could be a sign of pregnancy and should be checked by a doctor.
- If the type of contraception used needs changing.
- If there is a rash on or around the genital area.
- Any unusual lumps or bumps in the genital region should be checked out.

Confidentiality

Legally, it's doctors who have to decide whether or not someone under 16 is mature enough to make an informed decision about medical help. They'll decide this based upon the person's ability to understand what is being offered to them and their reasons behind wanting it. However, even if the doctor does say no, for example, to a request about the contraceptive pill, he or she has to keep the request confidential and their patient can go to another doctor or clinic for help instead.

Confidentiality at a GUM (Genito Urinary Medicine) clinic, for people who are worried that they may have a sexually–transmitted infection is stricter. Records kept at these clinics never become part of general medical records and are kept strictly private (so even the patient's regular doctor won't get to see them).

If you are at all unsure about confidentiality, it's your right to say to a doctor at the beginning of an appointment, "I want what I say today to remain completely confidential, can you promise that?"

Normal fears

Seeing a doctor of the opposite sex

The first thing most teenagers get embarrassed about is having to see a doctor of the opposite sex. If this is the case, you can ask to see a doctor or a nurse who is the same sex as you when you make an appointment.

Practice nurses (i.e. those who work in the doctor's surgery or practice) can also perform things like smears and answer the more embarrassing questions.

If you do have to see a doctor of the opposite sex, don't worry, they're not monsters. They've seen hundreds and thousands of male and female bodies and won't be shocked or stunned by anything you've got to show them.

Answering embarrassing questions

The next important point to remember is not to be put off by your doctor's questions. In order to help you, they often have to ask personal questions about your sex life and your body. These questions may seem nosy or silly, but they're important. Don't be tempted to lie, especially if you're being prescribed the pill, as a full family medical history is essential for this.

Asking supposedly silly questions

Being at the doctor's can be hard and confusing. This is why it's important to ask questions. Learn to be assertive and speak up when you don't understand what's being prescribed or talked about. Lots of adults are confused by instructions from their doctors, so saying you don't understand or need more help won't make you look childish.

Internal examinations

These are not as bad as they sound. A doctor cannot make sure a woman is healthy inside without doing a pelvic examination. This is a simple and easy procedure. The woman is asked to remove her lower clothing, including her underwear, and lie on a couch and raise her knees. A doctor will then gently slide two gloved fingers into the vagina and use his or her other hand to press down on the lower abdomen in order to feel the internal organs.

That seems fine...

Smear tests

Any woman who is sexually active should have a smear test every three years. A smear test determines whether there is anything wrong with the cells of the cervix (neck of the uterus). Abnormal cells are the first warning signs of cervical cancer but if caught early they can be treated with 100% success. The test is pretty simple. As with a pelvic examination, the woman is asked to remove her lower clothing, lie down and raise her knees. A speculum – a plastic or metal instrument (which looks like two long, flat spoons hinged at the handles) – is then inserted into the vagina so the doctor can reach the cervix. Then a thin spatula (like an ice lolly stick) will be used to scrape off some cells from the cervix for testing. The process is quick and painless and results should be sent through within three weeks.

Breast examination

Girls who get breast pain often need to be reassured that this isn't a sign of cancer. Breast pain occurs in most girls with growing breasts and usually occurs about a week before a period is due. Wearing a properly-fitted bra is the best way of dealing with this but a doctor can help if the pain continues. Above all, don't panic. Breast cancer (very rare in young women) is not connected to breast pain. However, every woman who has started her periods should regularly examine her breasts for any physical changes. The best time to do this is after the end of her period, as this is when the breasts are less lumpy and tender. Stand in front of a mirror and raise one arm behind your head. With the other hand, feel along the armpit and around the breast and nipple for any lumpiness or puckering. Most lumps are perfectly normal, but if a lump is new

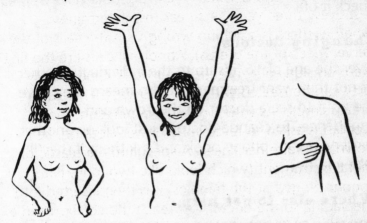

or feels different from normal, a doctor should check it out. Your local surgery will have leaflets available explaining self-examination in more detail.

Testicular examination

All men should regularly examine their testicles (balls) for lumps, bumps or changes in shape. The best time to do this is after a shower or bath, when the scrotum is soft and relaxed. Each testicle should be held between the fingers and thumbs of both hands and rolled between the fingers and thumb of each hand, to feel for any changes in shape, size or texture. Ideally, each testicle should feel like a hard-boiled egg without its shell.

Again, most lumps are perfectly normal, but if something feels new or not normal, a doctor can check it out.

Changing doctors

Over the age of 16, it's up to the individual whether or not they want treatment. It also means they have the right to see a doctor on their own and in confidence. To change doctors, just look up another surgery in your phone book and ask them if they'll take you on.

Where else to get help:

BROOK ADVISORY CENTRES – These offer young people free, confidential contraceptive advice. Brook can also help with emotional and sexual problems. They offer pregnancy testing and counselling. For more information and details of your nearest clinic, call Brook (see Resources).

FAMILY PLANNING ASSOCIATION – Family planning is free to everyone in the UK. The Family Planning Association (FPA) provides a national information and advice service on contraception and safe sex. They can also tell you where your nearest Family Planning clinic is. Most of these clinics run special confidential youth clinics. For more information call the FPA (see Resources).

CHAPTER SEVEN

Bigger problems

Deciding whether or not to have sex isn't the only dilemma people come across when they hit their teens. Once they've decided to have sex, they are at risk of a whole host of unforeseen problems, such as unplanned pregnancy or sexual infections. Even those who stay clear of sex itself may find themselves with problems of a sexual nature. Some may even be being abused or harassed in some way. Or perhaps they're unsure about their sexuality and are afraid to discuss it with someone. All these things can make people feel alone, scared or isolated, but help is at hand, if they only have the courage to ask.

Unplanned pregnancy

"It's stupid, I know, but I never thought it would happen to me. I had sex a couple of times without using anything and I was fine. Then I missed two periods and the next thing I knew, I was pregnant."

Shannon (15)

We didn't even DO it properly!

Most girls think that it will never happen to them, but every year nearly 8,000 girls under the age of 16 become pregnant. If you have had unprotected sex and have missed a period, it's essential that you visit a doctor and talk to someone you trust, your mum, your dad, or a relative. If you can't face anyone you know, then go along to your nearest Family Planning Clinic or Brook Advisory Centre and talk to someone there.

The first step is to get a free pregnancy test to find out if you are actually pregnant or not. If you are pregnant, counsellors at the clinic can then advise you on your next step: abortion, adoption and fostering, or having the baby. Decisions about whether you want to continue the pregnancy have to be made as soon as possible because if it is decided to have an abortion, it is important that it is performed early on in the pregnancy.

Abortion and the law

Abortion means ending a pregnancy by medical means. It is an operation during which the foetus is removed from the uterus. In order for an abortion to happen, two doctors must agree that a patient has grounds for it. This means doctors have to agree that their patient's mental and/or physical health would be at risk if they did not have an abortion.

Parental consent is not needed for an abortion for girls over 16. Under this age, doctors have to decide whether or not they think a girl is mature enough to make a decision about her pregnancy. They'll decide this based upon her ability to understand what's being offered to her and her reasons behind wanting it. If they don't think she understands, they will ask for parental consent. However, an abortion will never be performed against a patient's wishes. Even though abortion is allowed up to 24 weeks into the pregnancy, very few doctors now perform an abortion after 20 weeks. The later the abortion, the more difficult, risky and unpleasant it is, so quick action is essential once the decision to end a pregnancy has been made.

Post-abortion feelings

"I had an abortion three months ago. I know it was the best decision and I don't regret it, but I feel so guilty. I cry all the time because I can't deal with it."

Julie (15)

Any person who says an abortion is an easy option has obviously never spoken to someone who's had to go through one. Abortion is never an easy choice to make. It's a personal choice based on what is right for the person involved and no one else should try to push their opinion on the person making that choice – it's hard enough to make up your mind as it is. Most women who have had an abortion feel a mixture of relief, anger, guilt and misery. If you feel like this and can't get over what has happened, contact Brook Advisory Centres. Brook offers post-abortion counselling for anyone who needs it. The service is completely confidential.

Adoption

Some girls decide that they can't go through with an abortion, but nor can they bring up a baby themselves. In this case they may choose adoption instead. If you want to take this option, ask your doctor or counsellor to put you in touch with the Adoption and Fostering Department of your local Social Services.

Wanting a baby

"I desperately want a baby. I am 15 and I know I could cope because I love children. I want something to love and look after. My boyfriend is quite into it too, but I know my parents would go mad if I got pregnant."

Laura (15)

Lots of women find they have broody (the desire to have a child) feelings. They imagine a cute smiling baby who will make their life happy. If you think this is what having a child is like, take a walk down to your local park or supermarket and look at all the harassed mothers with their screaming two-year-olds.
Having a child is not a

solution to any problem. It won't make you feel happy, fulfilled and loved, especially if you don't feel these things already. Being a parent is a huge responsibility and will only make your life more difficult. Think about how much it will cost to clothe and feed a baby, and about where you'll live. Think about the child. Doesn't he/she deserve to have the best chance in the world? What kind of life can you offer it when you're still a teenager? And what about your life? You won't be able to go out so much, you'll have less in common with your friends, your education will suffer, and as result so will your chances of getting a good job.

As for the chances of your relationship lasting with a baby, studies show couples under the age of 18 who have babies are three times more likely to split up.

Too many partners?

"I've slept with about four guys. I hate myself for it because most of the time I don't really want to do it, but then they ask me and I think it will make them like me more, so I do it. Then I never hear from them again."

Jen (15)

Some girls sleep with a lot of boys, some girls don't. This is their choice and theirs alone. There is no such thing as a 'slag' or 'being easy' – these are abusive and sexist terms which means nothing. Girls are allowed to be as sexual as boys, no matter what some ignorant people think.

However, sleeping with a lot of different people does carry a huge risk. The more sexual partners a person has, the more likely it is that they will get a sexually-transmitted infection. What's more, someone who has sex and then regrets it on a regular basis, may need to question why they do it.

Remember:

Sex won't buy you:

- A boyfriend
- Happiness
- A fulfilling relationship
- Love

Sexually transmitted infections

STIs or Sexually Transmitted Infections (also known as STDs) are infections that can be passed from one person to another during sex. There are at least 25 different infections and these can be spread by vaginal intercourse and oral sex. These infections are called genito-urinary infections because they can affect the genital area, as well as the bladder.

It's important to realise that, if left untreated, sexually-transmitted infections can cause serious and permanent damage to health. Some can even cause infertility, making it impossible to have children.

Just about anyone can get an STI. Unprotected sex (sex without a condom) puts a person at risk of infection, because in most cases, it's impossible to tell whether someone has an STI just by looking. Lots of STIs have no recognisable symptoms.

Signs of an STI

Possible signs could be:

- Discharge that itches, smells or becomes thicker
- Pain when urinating
- Spots or sores on the vagina or penis
- Warts on the vagina or penis
- Blood when urinating
- Pain or cramps during sex

However, there are a number of sexual infections that have no symptoms at all. For instance, 9 out of 10 women with gonorrhoea (also known as 'the clap') don't get any symptoms, and chlamydia (see below) has no recognisable symptoms at all. This is because symptoms may be on the inside and therefore invisible to the eye.

Watch out for:

Chlamydia

The scary thing about chlamydia is that because people don't know they've got it, they don't realise they're passing it on. Department of Health figures show 36% of females with chlamydia are under 20 years of age, which means it's the most common, serious sexually-transmitted infection in young people.

Chlamydia is caused by a bacteria and is very easy to catch, especially if a condom isn't always used. Brook Advisory Centres say it can even be passed on by fingering (inserting fingers into the vagina). The only way to find out if you have it or not is to have a specific test at a GUM (Genito-urinary medicine) clinic. Once chlamydia is diagnosed, a doctor will prescribe a course of antibiotics, which will cure the infection in two weeks. If one partner is infected, the other partner should also get treated and both should stay clear of sex until the infection has cleared up, to avoid re-infection.

If left untreated, chlamydia in women will cause menstrual pain, pain during intercourse and severe PID (Pelvic Inflammatory Disease) which can lead to infertility. In men, it will also cause infertility. For an information leaflet on chlamydia, contact Brook Advisory Centres or the Family Planning Association.

Cystitis

Cystitis is an infection and/or inflammation of the bladder. It's one of the most common female medical conditions around and affects around 50% of all women at some time in their life.

The symptoms of cystitis include:

- a burning, stinging pain when you go to the toilet
- a constant urge to go to the toilet
- feeling unwell, particularly nauseous, weak or feverish

50% of all cases are caused by germs reaching the urethra (which is usually germ-free) and travelling up to the bladder, where they multiply and irritate the bladder lining. This occurs because a woman's vagina, urethra and anus are so close together that it's very easy for germs to spread.

Some women find that they suffer cystitis attacks after having sex. One reason is that it's easy to push germs into the urethra during sex. Perfumed soaps, bath foams or vaginal deodorants can also be to blame as they can irritate the sensitive skin around the vagina, acting as triggers for cystitis.

Another cause of cystitis is not drinking enough. Drinking frequently means going to the toilet frequently too, so urine will become more diluted. This means that harmful germs will be flushed out of the bladder. Having a more diluted form of urine means there is less chance of bacteria breeding in the bladder.

It's important to see a doctor when you first get cystitis, but an attack can also be relieved by doing the following:

- Drinking 300mls of water (just over half a pint) straightaway, then every twenty minutes for three hours, as this will help to flush out the germs.
- Avoiding alcohol and fruit juices, fizzy drinks and coffee.
- Going to the toilet as much as possible, not keeping it in.

- Holding a hotwater bottle against the stomach and lower back can help relieve the pain.

The best cure for cystitis is prevention. Do the following things daily to help prevent an attack.

1 Drink water. Drinking two litres or more of plain water every day will keep the bladder flushed free of germs.
2 Go to the toilet when necessary – don't hold it in (stale urine left in the bladder can make germs multiply).
3 Always wipe from front to back after going to the toilet to stop the spread of germs from the anus to the urethra.

Thrush

Thrush is caused by a yeast-like fungus that normally lives quite harmlessly on the skin, in the mouth and in the vagina. It is called Candida Albicans. If the body is healthy, it is kept under control by the presence of certain bacteria. Only when this delicate balance is upset does the fungus grow and multiply and cause discomfort. This can happen as a result of taking antibiotics. They don't affect yeast directly but they kill other organisms in the body, leaving the yeast more room to multiply and cause an infection.

Although thrush is often caused by the multiplication of yeasts, it is also possible to catch thrush from someone else. It can be carried by men without them having any symptoms.

The main symptoms of thrush are:

- itching
- soreness around the vagina and/or anus
- a thick white discharge that looks like cottage cheese
- pain when you go to the toilet

If you think you've got thrush, see a doctor. This is important, as thrush shares symptoms with other STIs and can be confused with them. Your doctor should be able to tell straightaway just by looking whether or not it is thrush. It can be treated easily by cream and pessaries. A pessary is an almond-shaped tablet which is inserted into the vagina with an applicator (rather like a tampon applicator).

What to do

If you suspect that you have a sexually transmitted disease, it is important to get medical help quickly. Go to your nearest GUM clinic, details of which will be in your local phone directory under G. Your doctor cannot treat you because specialist facilities are needed to test for STIs. However, you don't need a letter from your doctor to be referred, you can just turn up. Check-ups and treatment are confidential (your notes won't leave the clinic) and free.

HIV and AIDS

Despite recent advances in treatment, AIDS (Acquired Immune Deficiency Syndrome) remains an incurable illness, whereby the body's immune system stops functioning properly, leaving the body defenceless in the face of illness and infection. It is caused by a virus called HIV (Human Immunodeficiency Virus).

HIV can stay in the blood stream for up to ten years without any symptoms. However, during this time it can be transmitted to other people.

The HIV virus can't live outside the body, therefore to get inside the body it has to be passed through blood, or body fluids, like semen and vaginal secretions. This is why unprotected sex is so dangerous. The same applies to those injecting drugs and sharing needles. To help protect yourself, always use a condom and limit your sexual partners. Remember, you cannot tell by looking at a person if they have HIV.

You can't catch HIV from

- Touching
- A blood transfusion in the UK (all blood is now tested for HIV)
- Donating blood (sterile needles are always used)
- Being coughed on
- Kissing – you'd need to swallow over 500 mls of saliva for this to occur
- Sharing a cup
- Sitting on a toilet seat

Genital warts

Genital warts are caused by the human papilloma virus (HPV) and are sexually transmitted. In men, they are usually found on the penis and in women, around the vagina and cervix. They tend to look like small lumps and have a cauliflower-like appearance. They are currently one of the most common STIs with the latest figures showing 35,487 diagnoses in males and 32,185 in females with 29% of diagnoses in women under 20 years of age. As they are highly infectious it's essential to seek treatment from a GUM clinic.

QUIZ

So now you've read the whole of this book, you probably consider yourself fairly knowledgeable about the subject of sex, but are you? Try the quiz overleaf, choosing whether the statements shown are true or false and then check your scores to see how much you've really taken in. For the bits that still confuse you, read the relevant chapters (as listed) and remember that this book is a wise guide designed for reference value as well as reading. Keep it close, for when it comes to sex, you can never be too informed.

Bigger problems

1. Under 16-year-olds who want to get contraception can get it from their doctor without their parents' being informed.

TRUE/FALSE

2. All virgins have hymens.

TRUE/FALSE

3. Foreplay always leads to sexual intercourse.

TRUE/FALSE

4. A period is monthly bleeding when the womb sheds its lining.

TRUE/FALSE

5. You can tell if a prospective partner has a sexual infection because they will have red lumps all over their genitals.

TRUE/FALSE

ANSWERS

1. True. A patient's relationship with their doctor is confidential, however, a doctor may refuse to give contraceptives to an under-age girl if he or she doesn't feel she is mature enough. (See Chapter Six)

2. False. The hymen is easily broken through playing sport or using a tampon so is no sign of virginity. (See Chapter Two)

3. False. Foreplay is sexual activity that can be enjoyed in its own right, without necessarily leading to full sexual intercourse. (See Chapter Five)

4. True. A period is made up of blood and womb lining. (See Chapter One)

5. False. It is impossible to tell if someone has a sexually-transmitted infection, as many of these infections have no visible symptoms. (See Chapter Seven)

APPENDIX I
Sexual Harassment, Rape and Child Abuse

Sexual harassment is unwanted sexual behaviour towards another person.

"This older boy at school kept touching my breasts and pulling up my skirt whenever I walked past him. I didn't know what to do. I kept telling him to stop but I was scared. It got worse and worse and so I started bunking off school. Then one day our head teacher caught him doing it. She went mad, suspended him and got a local policewoman to come in and talk to us all about sexual harassment. Now I know to do something right away if someone touches me in a sexual way and I don't want them to."

Tina (12)

Sexual Assault is any kind of intentional sexual activity and touching without your consent. Under the new Sexual Offences Act 2003, sexual assault includes: being made to touch any part of someone else's body, clothed or unclothed, with your body or with an object; flashing and voyeurism (when someone takes pleasure from watching other people have sex). Remember sexual assault is never your fault, and though you may not feel you can go to the police it is very important to talk to someone about what has happened as the effects are far reaching. See the section at the end of this appendix for who to contact for confidential help and advice.

Rape is when a man (any man, even a husband or boyfriend) forces a woman to have sex against her will. It is also rape when a man is forced to have sex with another man.

Remember: No one asks to be raped. Wearing provocative clothing, walking alone or flirting are not invitations to be raped. However, being cautious is, unfortunately, a necessity. Everyone should be wary of going to places alone at night or visiting isolated areas. If you ever feel threatened, seek help immediately, even if it's a false alarm.

If you are the victim of a rape, remember you are not to blame. Report it to the police immediately. They are trained to be sensitive in this area and you will receive sympathetic treatment, counselling and medical support. Try not to bathe until you have been examined by a doctor – your clothes and body may hold vital evidence. If you need advice or someone to talk to, call the Rape Crisis number in your local directory.

Child abuse is when an adult or older person attacks a child in a physical, verbal or sexual way. Incest is when a child is sexually abused by a member of their immediate family.

Your body is yours and yours alone. No-one (no matter who they are) has the right to touch you, abuse you or hurt you in any way – no matter who they are. If any of these things have happened to you, or are happening to you and you can't turn to someone you know – a teacher, an older friend, a friend's parent, a relative, your doctor – then contact any of the numbers at the end of this appendix; they are all totally confidential helplines. You can also call your local social services for help; their number will be in the telephone directory.

Further help

(All services are totally confidential)
Childline 0800 1111 (freephone 24 hrs a day)
Careline 0208 514 1177 (counselling service)
NSPCC (National Society for the Prevention of Cruelty to Children) Helpline 0800 800500 (freephone 24 hrs a day)
The Samaritans 08457 909090
London Rape Crisis 0207 837 1600
Rape and Sexual Abuse Support Centre 020 8683 3300
Survivors UK (for men and boys who have been assaulted) 0845 1221201

Glossary

ABORTION
An operation to bring a pregnancy to an end by removing the foetus from the uterus.

AIDS
AIDS (Acquired Immune Deficiency Syndrome) is a condition where the body's immune system stops functioning properly, leaving the body defenceless in the face of illness and infection. AIDS is caused by a virus called HIV (Human Immunodeficiency Virus) which is passed through blood, semen and vaginal fluids.

CERVIX
The neck of the uterus or womb.

CLITORIS
A pea-sized organ found at the front of a woman's genital area. Its function is for sexual pleasure.

CONTRACEPTION
This is another term for birth control. All the many ways of preventing a pregnancy come under this heading.

CONDOMS

Also known as johnnies, French letters, rubbers and sheaths – condoms are a barrier form of contraception made of thin latex rubber. They look like long balloons and come rolled up inside a packet. They are designed to cover an erect penis before sex.

EJACULATION

The release of semen through the penis.

ERECTION

An erection is the name given for an aroused penis, i.e. a stiff penis filled with blood.

EROGENOUS ZONES

Areas of the body sensitive to sexual sensation.

FERTILISATION

When a sperm enters an egg and forms a new cell, which eventually becomes a foetus.

FOETUS

A foetus is the medical name for a developing baby in the uterus.

FOREPLAY

Foreplay is sexual activity that happens before actual penetration or intercourse. This can include kissing, hugging, stroking and oral sex.

FORESKIN

The skin covering the end of the penis. Some boys have this removed for religious or health reasons.

FRENCH KISSING
French kissing is kissing with open mouths, using tongues. What usually happens is, you open your mouth and insert your tongue into your boyfriend or girlfriend's mouth and vice versa. It sounds revolting, but it can be really nice with the right person.

FRIGID
A word boys sometimes use to insult girls who won't have sex with them. The implication is that the girl is too cold to have sex. There is no medical condition known as frigidity.

GENITALS
These are the body's sexual organs. For boys, these include the penis and the scrotum (the bag that holds the testicles). For girls, these include the vagina, the clitoris, and the vaginal lips (the labia majora and minora).

GUM CLINIC
A hospital clinic that deals specifically with genital and urinary medicine (GUM) and sexually-transmitted infections.

HETEROSEXUAL
A person who is sexually attracted to members of the opposite sex – also known as being 'straight'.

HOMOSEXUAL
A person who is sexually attracted to members of his or her own sex – also known as being 'gay'.

HORMONES
These are naturally produced chemicals from the brain.

HYMEN
The opening of the vagina is covered by a thin membrane of skin called the hymen. When you have sex, this hymen breaks (if it has not already broken) and some girls find that they bleed. Years ago, it was thought that the presence of the hymen was the only way you could tell if a girl was a virgin. Nowadays we know that the hymen is fairly fragile and can be broken easily through sport and/or the use of tampons, so it's no indication of virginity.

IMPOTENT
This means a man is unable to get an erection.

INFERTILITY
Someone who is infertile is unable to produce sperm or ovum (eggs) and is therefore unable to have children without medical help.

INTERCOURSE
Sex, penetration, making love, f***ing: these are just some of the other names given to intercourse, which is basically the technical name for having sex, when a penis is inserted into the vagina.

LESBIAN
A woman who is sexually attracted to other women.

LUBRICATION
Lubrication is a means of making something slippery

or moist. In sexual terms, the vagina needs lubrication to enable the penis to enter. This can be through the vagina's natural secretions or through the use of a man-made lubricant, such as KY Jelly.

MASTURBATION
This is rubbing, touching and stroking your own sex organs for sexual pleasure.

MENARCHE
A girl's first period.

OESTROGEN
The main female sex hormone.

ORAL SEX
Oral sex means using the mouth and tongue to stimulate the genitals of a sexual partner. Oral sex performed on a man is known as fellatio (or 'blow job') and on a woman as cunnilingus.

ORGASM
The peak of sexual pleasure, the muscles in the pelvic region contract and then relax, giving a feeling of release. In boys, this release takes the form of an ejaculation of semen.

PENETRATION
The stage during sexual intercourse when the penis enters the vagina.

PORNOGRAPHY
Pornography is the explicit depiction of sexual activity in films, books, magazines or photographs.

PUBERTY
The physical and bodily changes that happen to make girls and boys sexually mature.

RAPE
Rape is when someone is forced to have sex against their will.

SAFER SEX
This is sex that lessens the risk of contracting a sexual disease, for example, by using proper protection, such as condoms.

SEMEN
The thick, whitish substance containing sperm and fluid, which is ejaculated from the penis on orgasm.

SEXUALLY-TRANSMITTED INFECTIONS
Sexually-transmitted infections are also known as STIs. You might also know them as STDs (sexually-transmitted diseases) or VD (venereal disease). If you suspect you have an infection, it is important to get medical help quickly. Possible signs could be a discharge and/or itchiness, pain when urinating and spots or warts on your vagina or penis.

SEXUAL HARASSMENT
This is unwanted sexual behaviour from one person to another.

SMEAR TEST
A smear test is an internal examination which determines whether there is anything wrong with the cells of the cervix. Abnormal cells are the first

warning signs of cervical cancer but if caught early they can be treated with a 100% success.

TESTOSTERONE
The male sex hormone.

URETHRA
The tube through which urine exits the body from the bladder.

VIRGIN
A virgin is a person who has not yet had sex.

WET DREAM
The release of semen while sleeping.

WITHDRAWAL
Withdrawal is when a boy withdraws his penis from the vagina just before ejaculation. It is thought (wrongly) that this stops semen from entering the vagina.

Resources

If you need further information or advice about the issues covered in this book, contact one of the organisations listed below.

Acne Support Group
www.stopspots.org
Tel: 0870 870 2263

BPAS - British Pregnancy Advice Service
www.bpas.org
Tel: 08457 304030

Brook Advisory Centres
www.brook.org.uk
Tel: 0800 0185 023

Childline
Tel: 0800 1111

FPA (Family Planning Association)
www.fpa.org.uk
FPA Contraceptive helpline 0845 310 1334

Lesbian and Gay Switchboard
www.llgs.org
Tel: 020 7837 7324

Like it is - Marie Stopes sex website for teenagers
www.likeitis.org.uk

Men's Health
www.malehealth.co.uk
NAPAC - National Association for People Abused in Childhood
www.napac.org.uk
Tel: 0800 085 3330 (9am-1pm Monday to Friday)

National AIDS Helpline
www.nspcc.org.uk
Tel: 0800 567123

NSPCC
www.nspcc.org.uk
Tel: 0808 800 5000

Rape Crisis
www.rapecrisis.co.uk
Contains a list of telephone numbers for your area

Sex Etc.
www.sxetc.org
A site written for and by teenagers

Sexual Health Direct Helpline
Tel: 0845 310 1334

Sexwise Confidential Advice Line
Tel: 0800 282930

The Site
www.thesite.org.uk
Advice on sex, and contraception

The website addresses (URLs) included in this book were valid at the time of going to press. However, because of the nature of the Internet, it is possible that some addresses may have changed, or sites may have changed or closed down since publication. While the authors and publishers regret any inconvenience this may cause the readers, no responsibility for any such changes can be accepted by either the authors or the publisher.

Index

Wise Guides:
helping you deal with whatever life throws at you

Bullying
Michele Elliott

Drugs
Anita Naik

Eating
Anita Naik

Exam Skills
Kate Brookes

Family Break-up
Matt Whyman

Periods
Charlotte Owen

Personal Safety
Anita Naik

Self-Esteem
Anita Naik

Sex
Anita Naik

Wise Guide

BULLYING

Michele Elliott

Nearly everyone is bullied at some point in their life. But what exactly does bullying mean? Are there practical things you can do to stop it? How do you deal with your anger and frustration? How can you learn to make friends and respect yourself? If you're a bully, can you ever change your behaviour?

Don't suffer in silence. Learn how to beat the bullies and restore your self-esteem with this essential wise guide.

Wise Guide

DRUGS

Anita Naik

What are drugs?
What do they do to your mind –
and your body?
Are you under pressure to take drugs?
Do you have friends who already do?
What are the risks – and how should
you deal with them?

Alcohol and amphetamines, tobacco and
cannabis, solvents and steroids – know
the realities and explode the myths with
this essential wise guide.

Wise Guide

SELF ESTEEM

Anita Naik

What are you?
Positive bod or negative nerd?
Do you find it hard to take compliments?
Do you never take risks in case you make
a fool of yourself?
Then you need to respect yourself!

Anita Naik gives loads of helpful tips on
how to feel better about yourself and
build your self-esteem. Get in touch with
that positive bod that's just waiting to be
let loose on the world!